7-3-14

Bonnie,

Follow your Dreams!

Pocket Full of Dreams

A true story of self-transformation:
Overcoming abuse, poverty,
and tragedy to find success,
inner peace, and love.

DAVID B. BURCH

ISBN 978-0-9883778-0-6

Published in the United States of America

Printed by Color House Graphics
3505 Eastern Ave. S.E., Grand Rapids, Mich. 49548
www.colorhousegraphics.com

Edited by Christine Beyer Perez
Book design by Joseph L. Naimo, NīMō Studios
www.nimo-studios.com

This is a work of nonfiction. The experiences and events detailed herein are all true and retold to the best of the author's recollection. Some names have been changed to protect the privacy of various individuals involved.

AUTHOR'S NOTE

I decided to start writing this book on the eve of my 50th birthday. My prayer is that by sharing my story, others who are struggling or feel they have no hope, will see that life *can* and *will* get better. Maybe not today or tomorrow, but it will get better.

— David B. Burch

For Mrs. B., the keeper of my heart.

In Memory of
Sgt. Sean P. Luketina, 82nd Airborne Division
July 1, 1960 – June 30, 1984

Acknowledgments

I want to start by thanking my wife and children for their love and support.

Thank you to my brother Jeff, for always being there and for having my back.

To my parents... I know you loved me and did the best you could. I often wonder how different things would have been if alcohol had not been a part of our lives.

To my stepmother... your love and compassion has meant so much to me. You have been a true inspiration.

My deepest gratitude to my grandmother, aunts, and uncles, who cared for us when needed and who helped me during difficult times. A special thanks to my Uncle Bruce.

Thank you, Teri. Your love and support over the years has meant the world to us.

To Tricia, your insight and advice has been incredible. We are so grateful.

Thank you to my mentors in East Jordan... Ed Brzozowy, Jack Zoulek, Steve Carpenter, Larry Gee, and Edward Burrows.

I will be forever indebted to our editor, Christine Beyer Perez, who has been truly amazing and extremely professional. You have been a Godsend.

I would also like to recognize the professionalism of Joe Naimo, our graphic designer, and Gene Paskiewicz, for his artistic work and help on special projects.

Last but certainly not least, Neil. You took me in and put up with me, even when I'm sure I caused you a great deal of frustration. You didn't always like what I did, but you stood by me and helped me when I had nowhere else to go. Thank you from the bottom of my heart.

To my friends and family who were not mentioned in this book: Please know that it was not that our relationship was unimportant—because it was—or that my memories of you were not worth writing about—because they are. Over the past year-and-a-half, I've written far more than 300,000 words. This book contains roughly 60,000 words. It was a matter of editing and keeping with the storyline, with the goal of helping others who face similar struggles. I hope you will forgive me, and I hope you'll understand.

CONTENTS

CHAPTER 1

Liars

I was awakened by a commotion upstairs. My dad was talking loudly to my stepmother, Kathy, and I could tell he was upset. I looked at my clock radio; it was 6:10 a.m., and still dark outside. Then I heard my dad stomping down the stairs toward my room, yelling the whole time.

He shoved open the swinging bar room doors, which served as my bedroom door, and in one swift move, threw a bag full of garbage onto my bed.

The bag hit with such force, it bounced from the bed onto the wall and split down the side, releasing a heap of eggshells, coffee grounds, stinky beer cans, and T-bones from the steak we had for dinner two nights before. As I attempted to wipe the slime and grit from my face, neck, and chest, I recalled my dad's promise from a month ago.

"If you like the trash so much, maybe you should sleep with it!" he said. "The next time you *'forget'* to take out the garbage when you're supposed to, you *will* sleep with it!"

It took me a few seconds to remember that I had, in fact, forgotten to take the trash out yesterday.

It was the last week of school, and I still had one more exam to take before I would finish my freshman year at Trenton High School in Trenton, a blue-collar town south of Detroit.

I got up, turned on the light, and spent the next 15 minutes cleaning the disgusting garbage out of my bed. As I worked, my dad started in with his usual insults. His degrading comments were commonplace by now, but they still cut to the bone and formed the core of who I was. After a while, you start to believe the negative comments targeting your character and personality.

"You are a lazy, undisciplined loser, and you will never amount to anything if you don't change your ways," he said.

I picked up the six or eight beer cans first. That was about my dad's nightly intake on weekdays. On the weekends, it was more than that and usually included liquor as well. He was even meaner when he drank liquor. The trick was to try to figure out when Jekyll would turn into Hyde.

Next I picked up the steak bones, eggshells, and the soggy coffee grounds. There were also scrapings of old mashed potatoes, which had turned gray to match the rotting cobs of corn. I finished cleaning and went upstairs to take the trash to the dumpster at the end of the parking lot. We lived in an eight-unit condominium just off Fort Street on the south side of town.

I still had a mile-and-a-half walk to school and needed to get my sheets and blankets into the wash, plus prepare for the exam. I returned to the condo and headed up to the bathroom to take a shower. As I did, I passed my father, who couldn't resist a few more parting words on his way out the door for work.

Once out of the shower and dressed for school, I went in to the kitchen, where Kathy was fixing my breakfast. She set a plate of food in front of me and sat down.

"I tried to stop your father from dumping the garbage in your bed," she said.

"It's not your fault, Kathy," I said. "He told me a few weeks ago that if I forgot to take out the trash, he'd dump it in my bed. I was studying for my history exam, and it slipped my mind."

Kathy often tried to intervene when it came to the way my dad disciplined my brother and me. His response was usually to cuss her out and tell her to stay out of it: "You are not their mother!"

I finished my breakfast, grabbed my lunch, and said goodbye to Kathy. As I did, she told me not to let the garbage incident ruin my day.

"I won't," I said. "I'll get over it."

As I walked to school, my thoughts drifted. Not about the exam I was about to take, but of my childhood and the events of my life.

I have always had an uncanny ability to remember specific dates and experiences, even from a very early age. I remember Christmas of 1962, when Santa brought me a fire truck. It was the best! It had a ladder that moved from side to side and expanded up and down, and it had flashers and a siren. I was not quite 2 years old.

I remember having birthday parties at my grandmother's house in Flat Rock, Mich. My older brother, Jeff, and I always shared our parties because we were born 363 days apart. So for two days out of the year, we were the same age.

I recall the spring of 1963. My parents struggled, but did the best they could. One day, my dad's father, showed up, out of the blue. It was the first time I ever saw him—and the first time my father had seen him since he was 5 years old.

What I remember about my grandpa is he could tell great stories and had a lot of tricks, like taking a hankie out of his pocket and making a bunny out of it. It would come to life and run up and down his arm before sitting on his shoulder. I never figured out how he did that.

Me with Jeff – 1962

I also recall how he and my dad would go to the bar a lot and come home pretty fired up. And by fired up, I mean drunk.

(My grandfather was hired to paint a rooster on the side of the bar, probably to pay the tab. More than 20 years later, I drove past that bar on Telegraph and West, and the rooster was still there.)

We were living in Rockwood at the time, a town near Flat Rock, where my grandmother lived. Our house, which sat across the street from a Catholic church, had what seemed like a huge set of white stairs on the south side. They weren't enclosed, and there was no backing on the steps. I was terrified to go down them by myself. If I fell backward, I would go through the steps. If I fell forward, I would tumble to the bottom.

A boy who was about 5 years old lived next door. Jeff had gotten a tricycle for Christmas, and loved to ride it up and down the sidewalk in front of the house. He was only 3 years old, but very independent. One day, the neighbor boy came up and pushed Jeff off his bike.

My dad saw this happen but did nothing. At dinner that night, he told Jeff, "The next time he does that, you take your bat and hit him with it!" (He was referring to the plastic bat that was part of a Whiffle ball set).

Sometime later, the boy again pushed Jeff off his bike. Jeff looked around and grabbed the nearest bat, which was a not the plastic bat, but a genuine wooden one. He hit the kid across the arms. Needless to say, that was the end of the bike-pushing.

Shortly after, we moved again, this time to a place in Huron Township, north of Flat Rock. It was in this house that I would learn about domestic violence.

My mom was pregnant again. She gave birth to Jeff when she was just 15 years old, and I came a year later. This would be her third child, and she was only 17 years old. One day that spring, my dad and his father had been out drinking. My mom was in the kitchen when my dad arrived home in a foul mood. We could hear the arguing heat up. In an attempt to get away, my mom ran into the living room, where Jeff and I were. I didn't know why he was so angry, and why he kept calling her "woman."

"Don't talk back to me, *woman!*" he screamed, as he hit her.

She tried to avoid his slapping and pushing, but couldn't. He pushed her out the front door and she stumbled down the steps. Jeff and I pleaded with him to stop hurting our mom, but he ignored us. He was like a man possessed.

She was begging him to stop, *"Don't hurt the baby! Stop!! Please Stop!!"* As she regained her balance from the fall, he jumped from the porch and went after her again. He chased her to the swing-set, where she became tangled up and fell backward over a swing. Just as she fell, a police car pulled into our front yard.

The police had been to our house on several occasions already that spring. My parents' arguments would prompt the neighbors to call them, but never before had things gotten this out of hand. Both officers quickly jumped from the squad car. One ran to help my mother; the other restrained my father.

Jeff and I watched as the policeman gave my mom a hankie to wipe the blood from her face. We watched as my dad was placed under arrest. A little while later, we would drive to my grandparent's house. My mom didn't want to be alone. She was still just a girl, and needed her parents.

When my grandfather saw that my mom had been beaten, he was furious. It's probably a good thing that my dad was in the safe confines of a jail cell, because my grandpa was ready to tear his head off.

My dad got out of jail the next day, but we stayed at my grandparents for a few days. Then we all went back home. Dad seemed to settle down for a few months, and things were peaceful again.

My sister, Christina, was born on July 2, 1963. Jeff and I played outside most of the time, as my mom wouldn't let us stay in the house unless the weather was bad. By fall, my dad seemed to be drinking more and more. One day, Jeff and I were outside with him while he was painting the house. He would set his open beer down on the porch, and then go paint.

Jeff spotted the beer and said, "Come on, Dave!" We walked over to the beer. Jeff grabbed it, took a big drink, and handed the can to me. (Mind you, he wasn't even 4 years old yet, and I was still 2.) I knew what he was doing was wrong, so I said no. He looked at me, shrugged his shoulders, and proceeded to finish the beer himself.

We walked back over to the swing-set and sat down. A few minutes later, my dad walked over to get a drink. Realizing the can was empty, he went into the house for another. He took a few swallows, set it down and went back to painting. Jeff looked at me again and said, "Come on Dave."

Sure enough, Jeff grabbed the beer again—only this time it was too much for him to finish. We walked back over to the swing-set and watched as my dad returned for his beer. He picked up the nearly empty can and looked at it with a puzzled expression. Then he looked over at us. Just then, Jeff threw up.

My dad walked over to us and asked, "Did you drink my beer?" "No," Jeff answered. "No," I said.

"Get in the house *now!*" he roared.

Jeff fell out of the swing as he hastily tried to get out of it, and we both raced to the house. My dad made Jeff put his hands on the table and bend over. Then he took off his belt.

Whack! Whack! Whack!

"I *hate* liars and will *always* know when you're lying," he hissed.

Then it was my turn. Guilt by association, I guess.

In the spring of 1964, we had to move again. This house was off West Road and Interstate 75. I think my dad either drank so much that he couldn't pay the rent or he lost his job, or both. Either way, we moved into a house that was not fit for anyone to live in—especially three young children.

The house was very small. It had two tiny bedrooms and a common area that acted as the living room, dining room, and kitchen. It had linoleum flooring and ugly paper on the walls. We had electricity and a refrigerator and a space heater to keep us warm. But there was no running water. There was an old-fashioned pump at the kitchen sink and another out in the yard. My mom would have to pump it several times to get the water flowing.

There was no bathroom, only an outhouse in the back yard, which I was terrified of falling into. I was only 3 years old, and the giant toilet seat was intimidating. There was no heat out there. We had a large pot that we would use as a toilet at night, so we didn't have to go outside. For baths, my mom would haul a washtub into the house and heat some water on the stove.

One morning as I woke up and walked into the kitchen, I saw a mouse on the floor in front of the refrigerator. I jumped up on the table and screamed. My mom came out to see what was wrong, and I screamed as yet another mouse ran across the floor. Three or four more followed. My dad came out with the broom and tried to sweep them out the door.

The owner of the place would put his old cars and other junk next to the house. It was a fenced-in, makeshift junkyard. The fence was missing in some places, and Jeff and I would go in and play in the old cars. There were also piles of lumber in there.

One day, my father came home from work and saw Jeff and I running around in the junkyard. He saw that we each had long sticks and were running back and forth, side to side very quickly. We would swat the sticks on the ground and then retreat back at the same time.

My dad yelled at us to quiet down, and then he asked, "What are you two up to?" Jeff replied, "We are hitting a snake."

My dad sat his lunch pail down and came over to see. As he approached, he heard a rattling sound. Suddenly, it occurred to him what it was and he moved swiftly. He picked up a board and rushed over to us, and with one hard thrust he killed the snake.

"That was a rattle snake, and if it would have bit you, you would be dead!" he yelled. We were hauled inside, and off came his belt. "Don't you *ever* play in the junk yard again!"

Ford Motor Co. was building a new plant across the street from our house. They had a contractor from Texas, and my dad was pretty sure that the rattlesnake had hitched a ride on one of the trailers.

After a few months, we moved yet again. This time to a four-bedroom, two-bathroom home in Trenton, on Fifth Street between St. Joseph and West Road. We had never lived in a house this big before, or in such a nice neighborhood. The house was white, with a large, covered porch, and I loved it.

Jeff started kindergarten in the fall and my mom, Chris, and I would walk him to school, as it was near our house. Things at home seemed more stable, but I missed Jeff when he was at school. There was a neighbor boy named Jack Hardaway, and he and I spent a lot of time together and became good friends.

My dad got a new car. It was a tan Firebird, and he would take us out for rides in it. I remember being so happy. We would go on a dirt road and dad would fishtail with the car and us kids would squeal with delight. Once he pulled over to the side of a road next to a cornfield. He got out of the car and started picking some of the corn. "Dad, isn't that stealing?" I asked. "They ain't gonna eat it all!" he said, which confused me.

That Christmas was the best we ever had. Jeff and I got bikes, new clothes and shoes, and a bunch of new toys. We wasted no time, and headed out the door with the bikes. It was Christmas of 1965, and there was plenty of snow on the ground that day, but it didn't stop us. We rode those bikes for hours.

Things were great. My father still drank a lot, and he and my mom would still get in fights, but not quite as often. My dad would play these head games with us at times. He would give Jeff or me the butt of his cigarette and tell us to go put it in the toilet. We would both go into the bathroom just off the living room and try to smoke it, coughing and choking as we tried.

Once back in the living room, my dad would look at us and ask, "Did you smoke that?"

"No. No!" we would answer.

Off would come his belt and we were ordered to put our hands on the table.

Whack! Whack! Whack!

"I *hate* liars! You can never trust a liar!"

It took Jeff and me awhile to figure out not to lie, but eventually we got it. The whole set-up was a test to teach us not to lie. My dad knew full well when he handed one of us the cigarette butt what we were going to do with it. It wasn't until later that we figured out that it was the coughing that gave us away.

In the spring, my dad bought a boat, a 1962 Chris Craft. We'd take it out on to the lake on weekends. It was fun, but scary, because we would bounce up and down on the back seat when my dad would go fast. Sometimes it felt like I was going to fly right out of the boat. Dad had a thing about veering from side to side, just like he did when he'd fishtail in the car.

Later that summer, he would take us fishing, sometimes in the boat, and sometime along the Huron River near Willow Metro Park. We would stop at the store to get worms and kielbasa to use as bait.

My dad was an excellent fisherman. My brother Jeff was pretty good as well. As for me, I did not have the patience for fishing.

Jeff loved to fish. He would relentlessly ask my dad to take us. Finally one day, dad walked us to the sewer grate at the end of the block and said, "Go at it, boys!' I said, "We meant at the lake." He explained that since the sewer leads to the lake, there must be fish in there. So we dropped our lines and sat, waiting and waiting. When we finally went home, I told my dad that the fish were not biting today. "Maybe next time," said Jeff.

Summer was coming to an end and I was eager to start school. I would be a kindergartner that year! I could hardly wait. My friend Jack and I were going to be in the same class, so I knew that I'd have at least one friend.

Jeff was in first grade now, so he went to school all day long. Jack and I spent a lot of time together in the fall, but once winter hit, we did not see each other as much.

On Christmas, Jeff and I each got a teddy bear with a chain around its neck, plus a few other small toys. It was nothing like the Christmas of 1965. That following spring, my dad sold the boat, which made Jeff and me very sad.

A few months later, he and I were in the backyard playing. We had an alley in the back of our house, but we didn't have a garage like many of the other houses, so there was a lot of room to play. My dad was in the house taking a nap, and Chris was playing in her room. My mom had gone to get her hair done at the beauty salon.

It was a beautiful summer day, and it was getting late in the afternoon. Mom would be home soon to make dinner.

Suddenly, two police cars, one from the north, the other from the south, came racing into the alley and stopped about 40 feet apart. Two officers from each car jumped out and stood behind their doors with their weapons drawn.

Jeff and I turned quickly and raced into the house. As we did, we could see another police car coming to the front, parking between our house and the Hardaway's. Once we were inside, we yelled to our dad, *"Dad, Dad!! The cops are here!"*

He quickly jumped up from the couch and ran to the front window, then to the back door. By then another police car had parked at the end of the street. Dad paced back and forth frantically, lost it seemed. Then a black sedan pulled up and four men in suits got out. One raised a megaphone and ordered my dad to come out of the house with his hands behind his head and kneel on the porch.

He looked at us and told us to move back into the dining room and sit on the floor. We did what he said, but as soon as he went out the door, Jeff and I ran to the window.

I think the cops got spooked when they saw us moving inside because suddenly they were pointing their weapons at the house.

My father yelled, *"Those are my kids! Don't shoot! Don't shoot!"*

The officers ran up the steps. Two came in the house. Two handcuffed my dad and brought him back inside. They sat him on the couch. My dad asked if he could smoke. Someone handed him a cigarette and he sat there holding it, unlit, with his hands cuffed together. He was waiting for a match.

Jeff, Chris, and I were just standing there, not knowing what to do or what was happening.

The men were FBI agents. They informed my dad that he was under arrest for the armed robbery of 11 banks in Indiana.

CHAPTER 2

Ghetto Steaks

My dad's hands shook in the cuffs as he tried several times to strike the match to light his cigarette. Several of the agents were also smoking, and the room quickly filled up with smoke. I remember the sun coming through the window, cutting through the smoke and shining right on my dad's face... which was full of shame. I could hear the anxiety in his voice as he spoke.

I remember that my heart was racing and my throat was dry.

My dad asked if they could wait until his wife returned before taking him away. The officers wanted nothing to do with caring for us kids, nor did they wish to wait for my mother to return. The FBI agent told one of the officers to take us to a neighbor's house.

Just then, my mom pulled up. It seemed like the car was still moving as she quickly opened the door and jumped out. One of the officers stationed outside tried to stop her, but she pushed past him, practically knocking him over.

I could see the panic on her face. She was frantic and tears were streaming down her face, as she ran to my father's side, saying over and over again, *No! No! No! Please no! Why? Why? Why?!*

My mom's actions caused Jeff, Chris and I to become hysterical. We all started crying. We tried to go to my dad, but the agents blocked our path and wouldn't let us near him.

"Please let us through! Let us see our dad!" we pleaded.

My heart was sinking, and the magnitude of what was happening was indescribable.

My mom saw the panic on our faces and turned her attention to us. Almost as if snapping out of a daze, she ran to us to hold and comfort us.

The agents helped my father to his feet and escorted him out the door. As he passed by us, he turned to Jeff and said, "You are the man of the house now. You have to take care of everything while I am gone."

Jeff was 7 years old.

We asked my dad where he was going, and he told us that he was going to Indiana to visit our grandma. Although I wanted to believe him, I knew it wasn't true.

It didn't take long for my mother's family to arrive from Flat Rock. Everyone kept asking me if I was OK. I told them that I was, but I just wanted to be left alone.

They decided that it would be best if we all went to stay in Flat Rock, which we did, for a while, returning home when school started. I remember looking forward to getting back to normal... whatever normal was now.

The first day of school was miserable. A bunch of older kids pushed Jeff and me and teased us and knocked things out of our hands. They threw things at us, and did everything they could to make us feel like we were less than human... like we didn't deserve to be there. It was like a public flogging or hanging or witch-burning.

Jeff and I didn't rob the banks—why were *we* being punished? The kids would taunt us by repeatedly yelling, "Bank-robber, bank-robber... your daddy's a *bank-robber!!* We did not expect this and didn't know what to do.

But we never once cried. My father always told us that crying is for girls. If we cried while or after he spanked us or used his belt on us, he would call us a little girl. "You must be a little girl, cuz only girls cry. Men don't cry!"

I still remember the fear I felt every morning as I left the house and walked to school. It was not a matter of *will* we be teased and persecuted, it was *who* will tease us and *when*. The pressure was very overwhelming.

As soon as we left the house, I could feel the adrenaline start pumping through my body. I was in a state of heightened awareness, like a field mouse, looking around in fear, anticipating an eagle or a hawk swooping in for the kill. I would look at each person we passed and wonder, "Is this guy alright? Or is he gonna start something?"

"This guy is cool. He's safe."

"Oooo, this one could be trouble... "

Jeff and I would try to ignore the mean kids by walking a different way to school—anything to avoid them. It wasn't all of the kids, just a group of about 20, all who were older than us. Our friends would try to tell them to shut up and leave us alone, only to be brought into the fold. They, too, became the subject of ridicule.

This went on for several weeks at the start of my first grade and Jeff's second grade year. Christina wasn't in school yet, so she was OK. Finally one day, as we were walking home, Jeff said, "Dave, if dad knew that we were letting these kids push us around and pick on us, he would be really mad. He would probably call us a couple of little girls for not standing up for ourselves to these kids."

Jeff, Christina, & me in Wyandotte - 1968

With that, we made a pact to take control of the situation and any others that came up in the future. "I have your back and you have mine" he said.

The next day, two older boys started pushing us and taking our stuff. They were third grade bullies. Jeff and I looked at each other and knew we had to do something. That's when it all seemed to come out. A month's worth of anger, frustration and pain reared its ugly head.

Jeff and I took them down and started hitting them with all our might. The next thing we knew, neighbors were coming out to break up the fight. We didn't come out unscathed, but we did get the better of them.

After that, Jeff and I became pretty good at fighting and ignoring pain. We got into fights almost every day for about a week. When the other kids saw that we weren't going to take their abuse anymore, the teasing eased up. We started hanging out with some other neighbor boys, Ernie and Larry. They each had older brothers in middle school and high school, and they had our backs.

Things were so bad in school that we started to skip every so often to hang out with some older kids. We would go down to the

Huron River and break into the boats on the docks.

The older kids were more interested in the alcohol on the boats, but Jeff and I went straight for the food. It didn't take long for the police to figure out what was going on, and my brother and I would be escorted home in a cop car. This happened enough that we were on a first-name basis with the police. Other times we would go to Elizabeth Park and hang out with the hippies that gathered there every day.

Shortly after my father was taken away, I started having extremely vivid nightmares—not every night, but often enough. The nightmares were of animals, or monsters that would come out of the closet, the bathroom or under the bed. It was as if they were three-dimensional. I would be wide awake, not wanting to say a word, as I did not want them to know where I was.

My heart would pound and my skin would crawl. I was terrified when they would lunge toward me and I would scream at the top of my lungs, *"Help!! They are coming to get me! Help!!*

I would cry and scream until someone would turn on the lights. Of course by then, the beasts were gone. Because I was *sure* they had been there. And I knew one of these times, someone else was going to see what I was seeing.

Jeff and I spent a lot of time playing down at the railroad tracks with the older kids (fourth- and fifth-graders). We liked to put a penny on the tracks and wait for a train to come by. The penny would smooth out like crepe paper and double in size. We also liked to catch garter snakes and other animals, and smoke cigarettes.

One day, the train was passing by ever so slowly. The other kids jumped aboard. Not wanting to be cowards, Jeff and I did the same thing. (If you've never jumped on a train, you do it by grabbing the ladder on either side of each train car, pulling yourself up... and holding on for dear life!)

We went about 300 yards down the tracks and got off at N.A. Mans & Sons Lumber. The older kids picked up rocks and started launching them at the windows.

Being only 6 years old, I was petrified, but didn't want to back down. I couldn't let the other kids think I was weak.

Jeff and I tried hard to hit the windows like the older boys were doing, but we didn't have the arm strength. We heard the crashing and smashing of windows, but neither of us was successful at hitting any. Soon, all of the kids were scattering like rats. They took off in all directions. That's when Jeff and I realized that the cops were heading toward us. We ran as fast as we could down the tracks.

We knew of a hole we could squeeze through under the fence up the way, and just needed to go a bit farther. Each time I looked back, the cops were gaining on us. The railroad ties were the perfect distance apart for the stride of a 6- or 7-year-old—but not for grown men. I could see the concentration on the cops' faces as they tried to time their steps with the distance of the railroad ties.

We jumped from the tracks and over the stones to the edge of the grass. The fence was in view. The hole was only about 5 feet away—just a little bit farther. I took one more look back and the cops were right on our heels.

"Hurry, Jeff!" I yelled. He scooted under the fence first, and I quickly followed. We took off running, knowing we were in the clear. The cops would have to go all the way around the fence, and by then we would be long gone.

A few weeks later, we did the same thing again. Only this time, there were two cops waiting for us on the other side of the fence. We tried to run past, but the officers caught up and grabbed us by the backs of our shirts. I was scared, sweaty and breathing hard. They took us to the car and asked us "What were you *thinking?!*"

They wanted to know the names of the other kids, but our dad had taught us to never be a snitch, so we didn't tell. We told them that we did not know the other kids. They took us home, all the while threatening to take us to jail. My mom was furious. I'm not sure there was even any leather left on the belt by the time she got done with us. We were grounded to the yard for two weeks.

My mom was the ripe old age of 22, raising a 7-, 6-, and 4-year-old all by herself. Back when we had money, we had chicken, meatloaf, steak, and other good dinners. But now she was struggling, and there was less and less food in the house. My mom had to get creative.

Jeff had a name for one of our meals: ghetto steaks. It was a piece of bologna fried in a pan, usually with pork-and-beans or green beans. Some days, we only had rice with sugar and butter on it or really watered down soup—one can for all four of us. We were always hungry. The food stamp program was in its infancy and hadn't spread throughout the county; in our area, if you didn't have money, you didn't eat.

One day, Jeff came up with a brilliant idea. He and I walked across the railroad tracks to the Big Boy restaurant on Fort Street. As we approached, Jeff told me to be quiet, smile, and agree with everything he says. He would do all of the talking.

We walked in and he asked to speak to the boss.

"All this trash in your parking lot looks bad," Jeff told the manager. "What would you think if you drove up and saw all this trash in the parking lot? Wouldn't it make you wonder what the kitchen looked like? Wouldn't it make you wonder if the kitchen was clean?"

"Me and my brother would be willing to clean this parking lot for you if you would give us each a burger, fries and a Coke."

The manager went out and looked around. Then he looked at Jeff and me. "Deal!" he said.

We cleaned the parking lot on a regular basis for food, and we soon did the same at the A&W restaurant on Jefferson Avenue.

In the mornings during the summer, Jeff and I would walk to school for a free breakfast—cereal, fruit, and milk. It was the first time I ever had Fruit Loops, which are my favorite to this day. The school also had activities. I became pretty good at board hockey. The game was played on a flat board with wood on the sides of it. On each end was a small slot that you would shoot the puck in to with a small stick. We also played kickball and basketball. We played almost every day, and Jeff became very good at basketball.

At night we would have babysitters. My mom had a job at a small diner on West Road by the high school. Sometimes, we would go there while she worked. If we were good, she would give us a treat. They had doughnuts on the counter, under the glass on a silver stand, so the incentive was definitely there. I loved the chocolate-covered doughnuts.

It was during this time, from the time my father was taken until the end of that summer, that several babysitters—both male and female—sexually abused me. It went on for what seemed like an eternity. In reality, it was probably once or twice a month for several months.

One day, my mom found some *Playboy* magazines in the house

and asked where they came from. "The babysitters," I replied. "They bring them over and look at them."

"Did they show them to you?" she asked.

"Yes" I answered.

That was the end of the babysitters—all of them. For me, it was the end of the abuse. From then on, one of my aunts or uncles watched us, and if they couldn't, we were taken over to my grandmother's house.

One night on the way home from Flat Rock, my mom was pulled over by the police for speeding. Jeff, Chris, and I were sleeping in the back of the car. Once we woke up and saw the flashing lights behind us, the experience of losing our father came rushing back. We all panicked and started screaming repeatedly, and at the top of our lungs: *"Don't take our mom!!"*

The policeman had no idea what was going on, and why three children were reacting so strongly to a routine traffic stop, but he quickly let my mom go.

Early that summer we moved again, to Wyandotte, a community north of Trenton. My mother had gotten a job at a bar there and wanted to be closer to work. I'm pretty sure we had gotten evicted from our previous home. The new place was a big red house, again by the railroad tracks. We only stayed there for one or two months before moving into a garage behind a Polish lady's house. She had made the garage into an apartment, but it was very small. In the rafters was a tiny bedroom where us kids slept. The living room, bathroom, kitchen, and my mom's bedroom were on the main floor.

Things got real bad for us. My mom still worked late nights at the bar. There were nights she had to leave us home alone with Jeff in charge. It was terrifying. I was worried what would happen if the garage caught fire or we got hurt, etc. I also remember being so hungry. There were days when all there was to eat was a mayonnaise sandwich, or a ketchup sandwich. It is hard to split a mayonnaise sandwich 3 ways, and we always tried to let Christina have the biggest piece.

Jeff and I would steal fruit off the Polish lady's fruit trees, and she would yell at my mom for it. We also started going door to door asking for glass bottles. We would collect them and return them to the store for a nickel apiece. With the money, we would buy whatever food we could to hold the three of us over for the night.

Jeff had been held back at school, so we were both in second grade now.

Once winter hit, things got even worse—no fruit on the trees. Somehow, we made it through. But I will never forget the pain of being hungry.

As spring approached, my mom started dating a man named Neil. He was bald on top and had a goatee. We started to have food in the house, and Neil took us to the movies.

Neil had a friend who owned a cabin in northern Michigan, and he let us use it for a week. That was our first vacation and we had so much fun. One day, we drove to a town called East Jordan. While Neil had a meeting, we played on a train in a nearby lakeside park. He returned, and then my mom went to a meeting. After that we returned to the cabin.

We all loved it up north. We found cardboard boxes and used them to slide down the hills of long grass. We also had a lot of fun swimming in the lake. On the night before we were to leave, I got ready for bed and walked into the kitchen where my mom and Neil were sitting at the table. I felt something tickling on my arm. It was a giant spider—black and hairy. I almost soiled myself as I swept it off my arm. Neil stomped on the spider and tossed it outside as he laughed. He told me that if it had bitten me, my arm would have turned green and filled with puss, then turn black and fall off. Or I could have died.

I didn't know he was kidding. And that night, I had a nightmare similar to the ones I used to have after my father went to jail.

Even after the spider incident, I loved the Great North. Neil told us that in the winter, the snow gets so deep, it could cover your whole car.

Once we were back in Wyandotte, things were so much better, thanks to help from Neil. When school ended, us kids all went to my grandmother's house to stay for a little while. Next thing we knew, my mom and Neil showed up with a large U-Haul and the car packed to the top. We didn't know what to think.

Once we were on the road, traveling up Interstate 75, my mom told us that we were moving to East Jordan. Neil had gotten a job at the East Jordan Iron Works, and she had a job at Fern and Helen's, an East Jordan bar.

I was excited, yet also inexplicably sad. When we stopped in West Branch to eat, Jeff and I jumped in the U-Haul to ride with Neil the rest of the way.

CHAPTER 3

East Jordan

The trip took us six hours from start to finish. We arrived at our new home in the afternoon of a beautiful summer day. We all helped to unload the car and truck. Jeff and I were 8 and 9 years old and very independent kids, not afraid of hard work.

We finished unloading in the early evening, and it was time to set up the beds. There were still boxes downstairs, but they were full of household stuff. As for Jeff and I, we were done for the day.

The next morning we woke up and were ready to venture out. By this time in our lives, we were street-smart kids. We still had our bikes from Christmas three years ago, so we took off. Our new house was on North Street, a few blocks from the school.

East Jordan was a small town, with one school that housed kindergarten through 12th grade in two different buildings attached by a common corridor. There was one other building about three blocks away that was also being used due to overcrowding. It was a former Goodwill Center. This is where Jeff and I would attend school in the fall.

As Jeff and I rode our bikes, we came upon what seemed like a huge forest. Heck, we were city kids and this was all new to us! We set our bikes in some brush (we didn't want anyone to take them) and walked around between the trees. We came to the top of a large hill, which dropped off about 50 feet. At the bottom was a creek. Again, this was all new to us. We had never seen a creek before.

We spent hours looking around. Eventually, we got hungry, so we went back home for lunch. The bike ride took all of about 5 minutes. My mom was not happy with us, as she did not know if we were out causing trouble. She laid down some rules while we ate, but we only half listened. After lunch we were off again, this time heading in the opposite direction. We headed north to a hill that we could see from our house. It was heavily wooded, and at the top was a large silver building. We later learned that this was known as

Water Tower Hill.

We spent the afternoon exploring the hill. On one side of the building, there was an abandoned ski slope that had been closed for years. Over the next five years we would spend a lot of time on this hill, especially in the winter. It was great for sledding. It also was the perfect spot for camping in the summer.

When we got home, everything had been unpacked and put away, and it truly looked and felt like a home. Mom was cooking dinner. Although we had only been there for 24 hours, I was happier than I had been in many years. It was like a dream come true. I went to bed that night with a smile on my face.

The next day, Jeff went for a walk while I worked on my bike. I had to take a link out, as it kept coming off and the chain was loose. A little while later, Jeff came running back yelling, "Dave, come with me. These kids threw a stick at me!" We ran down to where three kids waited. One was quite large and looked to be about 15, (he turned out to be the same age as Jeff), one was on the heavy side, and the other one was about my size. As we approached, the largest one introduced himself as Brad.

"Who are you?" he asked.

"I'm Jeff. And this is my brother David. We just moved here from Detroit. "

I think Jeff thought it would scare the other boys to know we were from the big city.

Brad just said, "Oh, OK. You guys want to hang out with us? We could show you around."

Jeff and I looked at each other in shock. Where we came from, when you met new kids, there was usually a confrontation.

As for the stick, it turned out to be an accident. One of the other boys, Dale (the heavy one), threw it without looking and it just happened to land near Jeff. The other boy's name was Bob. We would spend the rest of the summer—and a few more—hanging out with our new friends. It went by fast, and soon it was time to start school.

For our first day, Jeff and I decided to wear our coolest clothes. My mom had bought us matching outfits a year before, when we still had a little money, and these were the outfits we chose to wear. The pants were dark blue bell-bottoms. The shirts were green paisley print with puffy sleeves with four buttons going up each arm. Each of us had a sash tied around our waist to serve as a belt. When we lived in Detroit, my brother and I always greased our hair with a dip in the front. We stopped doing this shortly after we moved to East Jordan, when we started hanging out with Brad, Dale, and Bob. For some reason, we were compelled to drag the Brylcreem back out and apply it for the first day of school.

During our very first recess on our first day of school at the Goodwill Center, what happens? A group of kids circled us, started calling us names, and the next thing you know, here we go again. A lot of pushing, wrestling, and a couple of punches thrown. I looked up and see Dale, our big friend from the summer, running toward us. The other kids backed off immediately. Besides being afraid of Dale, they were shocked that he was on our side. We all got in trouble, but that was the end of it. I later became good friends with everyone in the group.

As the school year progressed, we became more accustomed to northern Michigan living. We started to learn how to live a better life in a better way. We no longer lived in the bad part of town, on the other side of the tracks. There was no other side of the tracks in East Jordan. Everybody was in the same boat. Most of my friends' parents worked at the East Jordan Iron Works. If you take a look at the nearest manhole cover or fire hydrant in your community, chances are it was made at the EJIW.

East Jordan is a small, close-knit town on the south arm of Lake Charlevoix. It's not as touristy as some of the neighboring resort communities, but more of a hard working, blue-collar kind of town. It shows in the work ethic of the people. The way they help each other in times of need. It shows in its athletic programs, in which the town takes great pride. I credit much of my strong work ethic to growing up in East Jordan. There were examples of good people everywhere—people who worked hard for what they had.

My mom and Neil informed us that they were going to have a baby in the spring. We were all happy and doing well and it felt like we were a real family for the first time in my life. We had everything we needed—food on the table and a roof over our heads. My mom and Neil seemed happy and in love, and I felt loved, too. What more could I want? Life was very good.

That Christmas was special. It wasn't the presents, because we really didn't get that many—not like we did three years ago, after my dad had robbed the banks. It was the feeling of finally belonging, of being accepted for who I was as a person, and not for what my father was. It was the best Christmas ever, and I was so truly thankful.

My grandmother and aunts, Nonie and Sue, came to visit. My grandmother cursed Neil all the way up I-75 for taking her daughter so far away from home and, heaven forbid, to a place that had so much snow! But after spending a few days with us, she could see how happy we all were and understood.

Us kids spent hours outside sledding and skating. We learned about snowmobiles and skiing. We also learned about shoveling the driveway; I could have done without that lesson. The snow never seemed to stop. I think Jeff and I shoveled every day from December right through until the middle of March.

Because my birthday is Feb. 23rd and Jeff's is Feb. 25th, my mom had a party for us on February 24th. We turned 9 and 10 that year, and all of our friends came to the party.

On Mother's Day, May 13, 1970, my mom unexpectedly gave birth to twin boys, which she and Neil named Keith and Kelly.

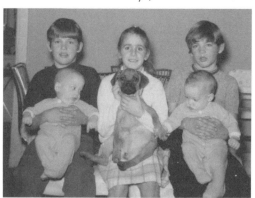

Me, Christina, Jeff, Keith, Puddles, & Kelly - Christmas 1971

Within a few months, our friend Dale nicknamed them Beeder-Deans, something he just made up. We shorted it to "the Bees," and still call them that today.

That summer, I spent much of my time with my friends on Water Tower Hill. Camping, fishing, exploring, and building forts became my favorite things to do. Our forts were amazing! We would dig a hole about three or four feet deep, cut down small trees with a hatchet, and lay them out over the top of the hole. We would cut off branches and layer them on, then add piles of pine needles. It all blended in with the ground, and we thought we were so clever.

My friends invited me to go to Little League try-outs with them. I was nervous, but tried my best. There was a long fly ball hit in my direction, so I dove for it and caught it! That one catch impressed a man named Jack Zoulek and he drafted me to play for the 10-12 year old league, even though I was only 9 at the time.

It was great because Jeff and I were able to play for the same team, which was sponsored by the East Jordan Iron Works. Jack was a big man, with a strong deep voice and a great passion for all sports, but especially baseball. He had three sons, John, Jerry, and Tom, who were all around our age and also played on the team. During the three years I played for Mr. Zoulek, I learned more than I did from any other coach that I've ever had. Not that I've had bad coaches, but Jack was that good. He took me under his wing and taught me so much.

I loved baseball and would be so disappointed when a game would get rained out. That first year, I started out in right field, then moved to left, center, and eventually second base. I also climbed from being the ninth hitter to the middle of the line-up. Baseball just came naturally for me.

Jeff and I also started playing football and basketball that year. During the lunch break, we played football, and after school we would play basketball with some of the older kids in the neighborhood. It was fourth grade and my brother and I were beginning to realize just how far behind we were educationally. I would have failed third grade if it weren't for summer school. I had to pass that in order to move on, and I did not want to fail. Failure is a word that is unacceptable to me.

Jeff and I could not read or spell well at all. Math was just as bad. When I got called on to read out loud in class, it was a nightmare. I think public humiliation was a motivational tool in the 1960s and '70s. Kids would laugh at me as I struggled to read out loud. I would look to see who was laughing, and get even on the playground. Most kids understood the relationship. Laugh at David for reading, and you will have a fight on your hands after lunch.

It was around this time in my life that I became more and more upset about the fact that I did not have a father around. Each year in East Jordan, they had a big father/son banquet. I can't explain the empty feeling this day would bring to me each year. It made me feel unworthy because I did not have a father at home, so I was not a member of the club. I was not good enough because my father was locked up somewhere.

I never asked Neil to take me because I did not know that you could have someone other than your father take you. I was an outsider. I just wanted to be normal. I told myself that someday, if I was ever a dad, I would *never* abandon my family.

Spring brought the Bees first birthday and soon baseball, which I loved. I was learning to be more confident in myself both as a person and an athlete. My mom got a third shift job at a factory in the neighboring town of Mancelona that summer. In the fall, we got a new (used) car. It was a Mercury Grand Prix station wagon and it had an 8-track tape player in it. My mom and Neil picked us up from school in it with The Jackson 5 blaring out the windows. I was so proud.

My personal life was going so well, but I still struggled with school. It was a constant battle for me to keep up with the other kids. It seemed like nothing came easy to me as far as academics. Education was not a priority at our house. We were never made to have homework time.

Jeff and I started going to Boy Scouts. The leader was a man named Steve Carpenter. He had two sons, Gerry and Duane, who were our age and we seemed to get along with them. Mr. Carpenter was the perfect fatherly type. He had a strong personality, was very driven and always gave excellent advice.

You know how when some grown ups try to give you advice and you just want to roll your eyes? Not Mr. Carpenter. His words seemed to come right out of a parenting manual, if there was such a thing. He looked after all of us, not just his own kids. He was fair and judged you for who you were and not what other people told him you were. He was the man, father, and husband that I wanted someday to become.

My brother and I loved sports. We would always go to the practice fields and watch the varsity team practice football. Soon all of players knew our names. We became the unofficial ball boys for the football team and later, the basketball team. Basketball started for us in fifth grade. We played on a team every Saturday morning and loved to compete.

That Christmas, we got our first snowmobile. Mom and Neil hung the key on the tree. When Jeff and I found it, we were confused until Neil told us what it was for. In the excitement, we ran out the door in our pajamas. It was a 1968 Johnson Ski Horse. Not the best sled, but we loved it just the same. We would ride it for hours until it ran out of gas.

Shortly after Christmas that year, my mom got into a car accident on the way home from work. The roads were very icy and she lost control. It was a really bad accident. Her face had been cut and required stitches. She broke her arm and collarbone and had a lot of bumps and bruises. The station wagon was totaled, much to my disappointment. That was one of my favorite cars ever. But it was a relief to know that my mom would recover.

One day, the phone rang and I answered. A man's voice on the other end said, "Jeffery?" I said, "No, this is David."

He said, "Hi David, this is your dad! How have you been?"

I did not know what to say or what to do, but I couldn't help but feel that this wonderfully happy family life that I had grown accustomed to was about to be disrupted.

Not long after, Neil moved out. I don't know what led to the break-up. My mom started going out with this guy named Bill. None of us kids liked him at all. My mom managed to save enough money to put a down-payment on a house across town. It was a small, two-bedroom house with an unfinished basement and a second floor. I was happy because it was right across the street from the Carpenter's house, and closer to my friends Al and Tim, and about a half mile from the Tourist Park beach. It was right at the top of the hill on M-66 looking down at the lake. What a great view! I loved it.

Bill was supposed to help her out financially, but he couldn't keep a job long enough. Neil had helped him get a job at the Iron Works, but he promptly lost it. Then he had a job at the plastics plant, which he lost within a month. He came over to the house crying about how everything was so unfair and people would not give him a chance. I thought to myself, "Well don't call in sick all the time, and maybe actually try working hard while you are there, and, *oh yeah,* don't get drunk every night and go to work hung-over!"

We got word that my dad was coming to East Jordan to help us move. This would be the first time we would see him since the police surrounded our house and took him away so many years ago. Jeff, Chris and I were very excited. I think Jeff was more excited as he saw this as a way to be let off the hook. He had never forgotten that my dad told him to be the man of the house.

I was looking forward to seeing my father, but was hesitant to have any expectations. By this point in my life, I had learned not to rely on anyone staying around for very long.

My dad arrived, with his new wife, Kathy. I was happy to see him, but did not understand our new family structure. It was all very confusing. My dad and Kathy bought Jeff and I new Spaulding baseball gloves. Mine was blue and Jeff's was yellow. They each had the outline of a white baseball in the mesh of the mitt. They were the first new gloves that we ever got.

My dad looked much different from the way I remembered him. The last time I saw him, he was just 24 years old. Now he was in his 30s.

Bill did not show his face the whole time my dad was there. I was kind of hoping that he would, so my dad could see what a loser this guy was and take care of him. Perhaps he would try to win my mom back, I thought. It didn't happen though.

Kathy seemed very nice. She was only 10 years older than me, and she seemed to really care about how we were doing. She spent a lot of time talking to us and listening to us, which no one else ever seemed to do.

Within a few days, my dad and Kathy left, and Bill started coming back around again. Our life was about to enter what I call "the Dark Ages," worse than ever before. My life would become more difficult than I ever could have imagined. The challenges I would face over the next several years would be unbearable at times.

CHAPTER 4

The Dark Ages

Bill was a very large man. He stood 6'6" and weighed about 235 pounds. Most of the time, his dark-brown hair looked like he had just walked through a Category 4 hurricane, and he had a beard to match. There were large dark circles under his eyes, and he was missing his front teeth, upper and lower. He looked much older than his 28 years. He was loud, uneducated, drank heavily, and couldn't hold a job. A real prize. He still lived with his parents in Grayling, about 30 miles from East Jordan.

Neil had moved out just after Christmas 1972. It was only a few months before this that Chris and I had started calling him "Dad." We had become very close to him, and calling him "Dad" just felt natural. He acted and treated us like he was our father. He was a hard worker, did not beat our mother, and came home after work.

The past three years of our lives, we had the stability of two parents who worked together to manage a household and provide an environment where we were comfortable, felt no fear, and did not go hungry. We no longer had to eat mayonnaise sandwiches, and it felt like we were a normal family. We even had two dogs.

Neil had given Chris a small, shorthaired dog for her birthday back in July. She named her "Puddles," because she had a lot of accidents on the floor. It was probably more our fault, not the dog's. Chris was only 8 years old, I was 10, and we didn't always remember to take her out. Chris loved that dog.

To this day, I cannot listen to The Beatles without feeling sad. They were Neil's favorite band. He loved "Hey Jude," and when I hear that song, it brings me back to the time when my heart was ripped out, once again. I never learned what happened between my mother and Neil, but within a week or so after he moved out, Bill started coming around. He usually showed up drunk. If he wasn't drunk when he arrived, it didn't take long for him to get that way. Having him in our home was miserable.

In mid-February, on an extremely cold night, Bill was walking into the kitchen in his stocking feet and stepped in a puddle of pee. He grabbed Puddles by the back of the neck and proceeded to carry her outside to the doghouse. It was much too cold for a dog to be outside.

"No! Don't make her go out there!" Chris yelled.

"Shut up!" Bill spat back. "Go to your room."

When he came back into the house, he said to my mother, "That will teach her to take care of that mutt."

My mom asked him if he would bring the dog back in later. He told her to mind her words—he was in charge.

Chris and I went outside in the morning to get Puddles. We found her, out of the doghouse, frozen to death in a pile of snow.

Chris was devastated. Bill appeared to be sober in the morning, and looked as though he felt bad, but he never did apologize. It was just one more of the many reasons why we all hated this guy. My mom tried to comfort Chris, but to no avail. Chris blamed herself, thinking that if she had just taken Puddles out, her dog would still be alive.

I tried to convince her that it wasn't her fault. It was Bill's fault for being so stupid.

Spring was approaching, and I was really excited for the baseball season. It would be my second year in the "majors," and I was sure that I could be the starting second baseman and Jeff the starting shortstop or third baseman.

Our first few practices proved that we had a pretty good team, but there were also other really good teams. The top three, EJIW, Rotary, and State Bank, would battle all year. The season was going well for both Jeff and I, and soon it was Memorial Day in East Jordan. All of the teams would put on their uniforms and march in the parade from one end of town to the other. We had the old gray cotton uniforms back then, not so cool when it was hot outside. It was fine with me, though. I loved my uniform and my team and was proud to play for EJIW.

After the parade, there were all kinds of events going on in Memorial Park. There was a tribute to fallen soldiers with a 21-gun salute, after a wreath was thrown into the lake. It sure made me appreciate our little town and made me proud to be an American.

After that, we headed to the ballpark for a double-header. It was a big day because we had an announcer and the field was chalked. It seemed like the whole town would be at those games on Memorial Day, and we felt like we were in the Big Leagues.

In the coming weeks, all the players started wondering about who would make the All-Star team. The team was usually made up of players in their last year of eligibility, but occasionally a younger player would make the roster, too. A few younger kids were invited to tryouts, including me. I was really excited and honored. I didn't make the team, but I knew it was a long shot. Jeff did, though, and I was very happy for him.

In the first game, East Jordan played Gaylord; we were considered the underdog by quite a margin. On the day of the game, we all piled in to my mom's '65 Impala. Halfway to Gaylord, our car broke down. A few minutes later, Coach Jack drove by and stopped. He took Jeff to the game while my mom, Chris, and I waited for Bill the moron to try to fix the car. The Bees were at home with a babysitter.

Christine, Jeff & me - 1973

Bill finally got the car started and we proceeded to the game, arriving just as it was ending. East Jordan lost by only two runs, but Jeff had had a really good game. He was so disappointed that we weren't there to see him.

With the season ended, we had the rest of the summer to enjoy. Jeff and I were offered a chance to go to Al McGuire's basketball camp at Oakland University. The cost for the one-week camp was $100 each. When we asked my mom if we could go, she told us to go to the payphone and call our dad and ask him for the money. Nervously, we walked down to the corner to the payphone at Lee's gas station and made the call, collect. He said yes! In July, we went to camp and loved it. We had so much fun and did not want to go home.

The Tourist Park beach was one of our very favorite spots to hang out. It was a small beach on Lake Charlevoix, and just about 300 yards from the baseball fields. Across the street was the Dairy Freeze. Much of the summers of my childhood and young adulthood would be spent at the beach in the years to come. It was one of my very favorite places to be.

Labor Day was upon us, which meant we would spend the night at a friend's house and stay up all night and watch the Jerry Lewis Telethon. It was the only time, back then, that the TV station would stay on the air all night long. That year, 1972, however, our attention was taken away from the Telethon. It was the XX Olympic Games in Munich, Germany. It was the first time I had watched the Olympics; it was also my first experience with terrorism. Terrorists killed eleven Israeli Olympians.

Sixth grade was our first year of organized flag football. We would play one homeroom vs. the other homeroom. We had two weeks of practice, and one game under the lights. It was the highlight of our fall. I don't recall who won, but we all played well and had a lot of fun. Football ended and basketball started. Once a week, on Saturday morning, we got to play basketball. Jeff was a lot better than anyone else in our grade, by far. Sports were a way for Jeff and me to escape our otherwise very depressing life. Bill was coming over more and more, and my mom had taken up drinking on a regular basis.

A few weekends a month, we would go to Bill's parent's house, a two-bedroom trailer. That's where Bill lived when he wasn't invading our home. The adults would sit around the kitchen table with half-gallons of Kessler's or Seagram's Seven Crown or both. There was always beer and heavy smoking. The trailer would be filled with smoke, especially in the winter. They would play cards and basically drink all day and into the night. Then we would all pile into the Impala (and by all, I mean Bill, Mom, Jeff, Chris, Keith, Kelly, and I) and Bill would drive us 30 miles back to East Jordan.

Us kids usually slept on the way home. One Saturday night, I was falling asleep and could feel something different about the car. I woke up to us sliding out of control and looked up as we slammed into a large snow bank. Lucky for us, the snow bank was there, because just beyond it was a drop off into a heavily wooded area.

I don't know how fast we were going, but now we were stuck on top of a snow bank with the back tires off the ground.

Bill staggered out of the car and tried to figure out how to get us down. Pretty soon a pick-up stopped and offered us a pull out. Bill gave the guy a couple bucks and thanked him and we were on our way.

Things were getting worse at home. We had managed to get on welfare, though; if it weren't for that, we would have had nothing. Powdered milk and powdered eggs are not the tastiest, but it was better than starving. (Certainly better than a mayonnaise sandwich split three ways.)

We got that, plus sugar, flour, oatmeal, and other staples from the welfare station. My mom also got food stamps. We got free hot lunch at school. I was very ashamed and embarrassed for my family. We were not normal. I had a quarter that I kept in my pocket for the entire sixth grade year. While we were in line for lunch, I would take it out of my pocket and fiddle with it while talking to the other kids. I really believed that they would see the quarter and think that I was paying for my lunch with it. But it always went back in my pocket until the next day.

For Christmas that year, we got very little. From my aunts and grandmother, we got socks, underwear, a shirt, and a new pair of pants, but there was little else under the tree or in our stockings. (That was really the only time we got new clothes.) The year before we got a snowmobile (for which we could no longer afford the gasoline needed to run it) and B-B guns. I could only wonder, "Was I really that bad this year? Why was our family so bad? Why do bad things always happen to us?" Even though I realize now that it didn't make sense, at the time I was convinced that it was me—I did not deserve to be happy or normal.

I remembered watching *The Little Drummer Boy* on TV just a few weeks before that. It got to the part where the drummer boy has nothing to give to The Baby Jesus, so he decided to play his drum for Him. I wanted to burst out in tears. (But remember, men don't cry.) I was overcome with sadness, thinking, "If Jesus were to come here today, I could not give him a gift or even play a drum from Him."

Earlier in the school year, we were given the opportunity to take band class. We could not afford an instrument, so I asked my mom if I could play the drums. All I would need is a wood pad with rubber on it and a set of sticks. She said no. We didn't have any extra money. I had nothing to offer. It was a very empty feeling for an 11-year-old.

Earlier that year, I started going to church with a few of my friends, Keith and Brenda. Their aunts would pick me up and give me a ride. Keith and Brenda's father was Larry Gee, a teacher and a coach at our school. Like Mr. Carpenter, he was a man of solid character who offered great advice. I wanted so desperately to be loved and have a father like him who taught me things.

Seeing how other families interacted and being invited into their homes made me realize just how dysfunctional my family was. However, it also gave me a chance to see that life can be better. In church, the seed was planted in me that you could make choices in life. You can do better and be anything that you want to be, that things will always get better—no matter how bad it is in your darkest hours.

I used to pray to God for my mom and my family, to help us be strong, to help me to stay strong, and especially to help me in school, as I still really struggled. I also prayed that Bill would just go away.

By spring of 1973, my mom and Bill were in a serious relationship. Jeff started hanging out with an older crowd and was drinking and using drugs on a small scale. My mom was spending more time out at night and on the weekends. Jeff and I were becoming the primary caregivers to the twins more and more each week. My grandfather died that year, and mom and Bill went to Flat Rock for the funeral. Neil came to stay with us for a few days. Apparently, Bill did not make a very good impression on my grandmother, because she told him that he was not welcome in her house ever again.

Things at home continued to deteriorate. We had not been able to afford to get our hair cut for months, and it was becoming long and shaggy. We were growing out of our clothes, which often went unwashed. My mom had been drinking more and staying out later. Many times, Jeff and I would wake up to the smell of smoke and the sound of loud music and laughing. My mom would have her girlfriends and strange men over. I am sure they were regulars at the bar, but they were strange to us.

One particular time, she brought home two strays. One was fresh from Vietnam. He wore an Army coat and was unshaven for what appeared to be many days. They were rolling what looked like cigarettes at our kitchen table and drinking whiskey. It was around 3 a.m. While Jeff and I stood there watching, my mom, in a drunken stupor, informed everyone that, "These are my boys. I am *sooo* proud of them. They are good athletes ..." and so on.

The Vietnam dude was really scary. Jeff told everyone that he would like to join the Army and go to Vietnam. My mom flipped out. *"Don't ever say that! Never! You will never go over there!"*

The scary vet told Jeff that it was hell on earth, and that he would not wish it on his worst enemy. With that, Jeff and I returned to our bedroom. I asked Jeff what was in the bag that they were making cigarettes out of. I had never seen marijuana until then.

"Dope" Jeff replied.

"What?" I asked.

"Pot!"

Although I didn't totally understand what that meant, I knew that "pot" was a drug.

I went to bed thinking, "How did all this happen to us? And how will it stop? *Can* it stop?'

A few nights later, Jeff, Chris and I were in the living room watching TV. I saw my mom pull into the driveway and then Bill pulled in right behind her. I didn't think anything of it until I heard the yelling. We all jumped up to see Bill slapping my mom as she struggled to escape. I couldn't make out what they were saying, even though they were yelling loudly. He was really violent and hit her time after time. Jeff and I ran to the kitchen and out the door toward them to try to help. Christina was crying and screaming. As we made our way out the door, my mom somehow broke free. Bill stumbled as we all ran into the house and my mom locked the door. He stood on the porch and yelled and ordered her to open the door. She refused, and eventually he got in his car and sped off.

At least I had baseball. I was really excited to play this year—my last year of eligibility for Little League. We had a solid season, and I was once again invited to try out for the All-Stars. This time I made it!

Sadly, right before the start of All-Star season, one of our teammates tragically died. His name was Bob Hopper and he was one of our best players. He drowned in a pond near his home. We were all devastated. I had never known someone so young, someone my own age, to die before. It hit me real hard. The All-Star game was played in Bob's honor.

I played third base and was given the nickname "Aurelio Rodriguez," after the third baseman for the Detroit Tigers. He had long dark hair that flowed from his hat, as did mine. We won our first game with ease, but so did Gaylord. We would face them next. They were still the team to beat, but we thought we could take them. We went to the top of the sixth inning with a 2-1 lead and were playing strong, when the wheels started to come off. We gave up two runs and went to the bottom of the sixth down 3-2. We did get a hit or two back, but were unable to score. Our season came to a bitter and abrupt end. Gaylord went on to the state semi-finals or finals or something like that. Although it was disappointing, life would go on.

We were heading into 7th grade, the year when flag football is replaced with tackle football! On the first day of practice, they lined us all up in the locker room in our underwear. This was a new experience. I figured the doctor would start at the beginning of the line and check everybody's mouth, ears, eyes, nose, listen to heart, lungs, etc. He did all of those things, but then came the infamous words: "Drop 'em, turn your head, and cough."

CHAPTER 5

Mom

After that unpleasant experience, we were issued our equipment, and the fear turned into fun. We were all excited about football. I got jersey No. 55 and my friend Versile got No. 44. He was a left linebacker and I was right. He was halfback and I was fullback.

Coach Larry Gee was a great man for the job. The first game was at Boswell Field on a cold rainy day. We didn't care—it was football! Heck, we played on the playground in the snow, so what's a little rain?

We lost the game 22-8. I thought we played well, considering that we were up against a private school, Traverse City St. Francis, from a town that was probably 10 times bigger than ours. Jeff and I had to miss the second game, because my mom made us go and visit Bill that day. We were very unhappy about this. What bothered me the most is that we were missing something that was good for us. Instead, we were going to a place where everyone would be smoking and drinking and doing drugs.

I played on the seventh grade basketball team that year and so did Jeff. Things at home were worse than ever. The abuse from Bill was happening on a daily basis. This guy had huge hands. He loved to grab us by the back of our neck and squeeze with the force of a hydraulic vice. At times it felt like my head would pop right off. When he grabbed our necks, he would shake us from side to side to make it hurt even worse. Other times he would backhand Jeff or me just for the heck of it. Did I mention the size of this guy's hands?

Bill did everything in his power to let us know that we were not in charge—he was. He went out of his way to make it clear to us that we were an inconvenience to him and in the way of his relationship with our mother. He would put his ugly face right in ours and tell us what he thought of us.

My mom didn't know this was going on, because he never seemed to do it in front of her. Still, she started to become more violent toward us as well. If we did something wrong, she would use whatever was in her hand, or grab the nearest utensil—be it a wooden spoon, plastic spatula, belt, it didn't matter—and start swinging. Sometimes you got it in the leg, sometimes the back, but she always got her point across. I don't know, maybe it was that we were at that age when we became more challenging or difficult, but whatever it was, there was plenty of violence in our house. Her drinking was becoming out of control, and it was almost like she was a different person.

I could not understand that if a man was a real man, how could he hit a woman or child. How could he hit the woman he claims to love? I did not get that. I made a promise to myself that I would *never* hit my wife, or any other girl. I would *never* hit my kids or any other child.

One afternoon, Bill came over, drunk and, for some reason, very angry. He and my mom were in the kitchen; Jeff and I were watching TV in the living room. Bill was yelling and my mom was trying to settle him down. We heard him hit my mom, and we both got up and ran into the kitchen. Jeff yelled at Bill to stop.

Bill lunged toward us and stumbled as he did. Jeff and I took off running. Bill was not far behind. By the time we got most of the way up the steps, he was right on us. In one quick move, Jeff spun around and kicked Bill square in the chest, knocking him all the way down the steps and into the door at the bottom. Jeff and I got into our room, closed the door, looked at each other and started laughing. What joke this guy was.

After a few minutes, we heard him go back into the kitchen and resume yelling at my mother. Jeff and I went back downstairs and into the kitchen. Bill turned and glared at us and said to Jeff, "You ever do that again, and I'll..." He punched what he thought was the wall but it was actually the chimney, very hard! The wall was all painted the same, but one part was drywall and the other part was chimney. He instantly doubled over in pain. Then he started crying and got into his car and left. "Fool", said Jeff.

We didn't see him for several days, but when we did, he was in a cast. Ha, ha, ha! Jeff and I got a kick out of that.

Jeff had gotten a dog for Christmas two or three years before. The dog's name was Spirit, and he was so sweet. He slept at the foot of Jeff's bed in our room every night. Jeff chose the name Spirit because he wanted to always be reminded of the Christmas Spirit.

One day, Jeff and I were walking home on a beautiful sunny day. It was about 60 degrees. We both had spring fever and were tired of riding the bus. There was still snow on the ground, but it was melting.

Jeff and I were hopping over the water streams that had formed in the street. When we got home, Bill's car was in the driveway. My mom was not home. It was the day that she had to go to Charlevoix to get food stamps and welfare food. As we were approaching the house, we heard a gunshot blast, followed by the sound of a dog yelping. We just stood there, stunned. There were woods behind the house on our acre-and-a-half of land. Jeff said that there must be hunters out, and we opened the door to go into the house.

Usually Spirit would greet us, happy to see us, with his tail whipping back and forth. Jeff looked around and asked if I had seen Spirit outside. I told him I hadn't. From the window, we could see Bill walking toward the house with a rifle in his hand. Jeff and I ran outside to Bill.

"Dog attacked me, so I had to put him down," Bill said. Then he laughed.

He did not keep a shotgun at our house, so he had to bring it from his place in Grayling. He drove all the way over for the sole purpose of shooting Jeff's dog.

Jeff was furious and started yelling at Bill. *I will kill you, you piece of crap!* Bill left. My mom came home an hour or so later. Jeff was still crying and ready to take Bill out.

Jeff and I got the shovel and headed into the woods to find Spirit. He was lying in a pile of bloody snow. We took turns digging a hole in the still partially frozen ground and buried him, then headed back home.

My mom and Bill were planning on getting married, although no date had been set. She told us of her plans, and we were devastated. Jeff and I hated him with every fiber of our being. I really hated to think what would happen if they got married. Would we have to live in Grayling and not East Jordan? If we moved to Grayling, we'd be uprooted yet again, and taken away from everything that was going well in our lives. We would be stuck in an environment that was many times worse than we had ever seen before.

But if they chose to stay in East Jordan and Bill moved in permanently, it would mean more partying and fighting here.

What kind of life would this be? The scenario had no good outcome.

Around that time, my mom told me about her relationship with my father, and how she had met him in the fall of 1958. She was a freshman and my dad was a senior at Flat Rock High School. My dad was in a group of friends with my Aunt Vivien. My mom told me that when she was 14, they started going steady. Things moved fast. They spent every spare minute together by going to movies, bowling or just hanging out at the M&M, the local diner.

About a month before her 15th birthday, she became pregnant. They got married in November 1959. My brother Jeff was born on February 25, 1960. I came less than a year later, on February 23, 1961.

She told me how much she regretted not being able to go to her prom or high school football games or just things that kids did.

My mother with Keith and Kelly

She was also disappointed that she did not get to go to college or have a high school diploma. She told me to be careful around girls and to wait to have sex. She told me not to do what she and my dad did. It made me think about all of the sacrifices my parents had to make.

Around Easter, we hadn't seen Bill for a few weeks, which was just fine with my brother and me. Once or twice a month, my mom would not come home at night. She would stay at her friend Helen's house in Boyne City if she had too much to drink. Jeff or I would stay home from school to watch Keith and Kelly; the twins were only 3 years old and couldn't be left alone.

On the morning of April 29, 1974, Jeff, Chris and I got up for school. My mom was not home, so Jeff said he'd stay to watch the Bees. He and I tried to take turns, as we did not want to fail the seventh grade, and I had stayed home last time. I already had six absences that year, and Jeff had at least five. Jeff started getting breakfast ready for the Bees, and Chris and I got on the bus and went off to school.

During second period, the school's principal, Mr. Shields, came in and talked with my teacher. After a brief conversation, they called me out to the hallway. I tried to review the past few days to figure out why I might be in trouble, but could not come up with anything.

Mr. Shields and I walked to his office, but he did not say a word. When we got to his office, there sat Neil, and he did not look happy. He shook Mr. Shields' hand and said thank you, and then turned to me and said, "Let's go." I was so confused. I didn't know what was happening.

I saw Neil's Mustang in the parking lot, and Chris was in the front seat. My first thought was, "Chris never gets into trouble. What's going on??"

On the drive home, all I could come up with is that we were moving to Grayling to live with Bill. That was how things worked. We were never consulted. We just loaded up and moved. I kept telling Neil, 'I'm not going to Bill's house. *No way* am I going to Bill's house!' My mom had been telling us that it would happen soon. *"I am not going!"* I repeated.

Neil did not say a word as he drove the short route to our home. Once we pulled in the driveway, I noticed a sheriff's car parked there. The Rev. Dale Turner's car was also there. Now I was really confused. Neil stopped the car and we all got out.

I could see through the kitchen window that Jeff was sitting at the table, crying and talking to someone. Neil turned to Chris and me and said, "Your mom has been in a car accident. Chris, Dave... your mom is dead"

I said, "My mom's head? What??" He said, "No Dave. She is dead."

My mind went blank and my heart sank. And then it raced. Chris started hysterically crying. Neil hugged her and walked her into the house. I just stood there for a minute or so. Then I walked around outside for a few minutes all by myself. I kept thinking, *"What?? How? How has this happened to me??"*

My dad always said, men don't cry. So I gathered myself and walked in calmly, trying to make sense of it all.

Once inside, I could see that Jeff was very upset. Chris was out of control. The Bees were running around as if nothing happened. Rev. Turner came up to me and asked if I wanted to pray. "No," I replied. He hugged me and told me that he was there for me.

At this point, I was very angry with God. Why us? What did we do to make Him hate us? How could He do this to five children?

The pain just kept coming. It seemed every time I got myself back up and brushed off, I would get kicked in the teeth and knocked back down again. I did not buy the whole "God will not give you more than you can handle" crap. "Just leave us alone, God," I thought. "I am tired... really, really tired."

I walked over and picked up the Bees and sat at the table, still not shedding a tear. "Men don't cry," I kept thinking.

It was chaos in the kitchen, so I took the Bees into the living room and turned on *Sesame Street* for them. We sat on the couch and watched Big Bird, Bert and Ernie, and Oscar the Grouch. People kept coming in and asking me if I was OK. I told them I was fine. I just wanted to be left alone with my brothers to think. I was over-whelmed with worry—what would happen to us?

And I couldn't help thinking about the events of the night before. My mom told us that she was going out with Helen and her friends. It was her night off, and she usually spent it with us. Jeff was mad at my mom and snapped at her, "This is our family night. Why are you leaving?" My mom said she had already made plans and that we'd have to watch the Bees and Chris while she went out. Mom and Jeff got into a big argument, and just as my mom was leaving, Jeff yelled out, "*I hate you!!!*"

Those were the last words he ever spoke to her.

I should have intervened before she left, made Jeff take it back and apologize. But instead, I said nothing. I would regret this for the rest of my life.

I told Neil that I was going for a walk. I just needed to get out of the house for a while. I walked to the beach at the Tourist Park and sat on the swings and cried... it was just me and Lake Charlevoix, and my grief.

"Why? Why do bad things always happen to us?" I thought.

I looked up for answers. The sky was very blue, with several large puffy clouds. One of them caught my eye. As I stared at it, I could see my mother, blowing a kiss and waving goodbye. I took it to mean that my mom was on her way to heaven.

I know my mom deeply loved us. Toward the end of her life, she started hanging around the wrong crowd and drinking too much, but she did love us and spent time with us. On Saturdays, when she was doing laundry and cleaning the house, she would put on *American Bandstand* and *Soul Train.* She loved to dance and loved to teach us to dance. She would grab my hand and pull me off the couch.

"Let's shake it!" she'd say, and we would spend the song dancing. She'd dance with Jeff, then Chris, then me again. A few times she would pack a picnic lunch and we'd spend the afternoon at a park. I loved doing that.

After a good cry, where no one could see me, I got up off the swings and started walking home. When I got near the softball fields, I could see someone walking toward me. It was my friend Jeff—one of the boys I had gotten into a fight with on my first day of school in the third grade. He came up and said hello and asked how I was doing.

He looked very upset and told me that there had been an announcement at school about my mom. He said that everybody was very sad. He said that he decided to walk home instead of riding the bus, because he wanted some time to himself. He could barely speak, but told me how sorry he was and invited me to his house anytime I needed to get away. We sat on the park picnic tables and just talked for a while.

I told him that I needed to get home, and he said, "Take care, Dave. Call me if you need anything." With that we parted and I walked the rest of the way home.

As I started up the hill, I could see another friend, Tim, walking on the trail toward my house. He told me he was coming over to see if we needed anything. I said no, and he told me how sorry he was as he turned to leave.

This is how people in East Jordan are. They want to help. They stick together when times are hard.

When I arrived home, my grandmother and other family members were there. Grandma came to me with tears streaming down her cheeks and hugged me. I hugged her back, then went to my bedroom.

I turned on the radio and crawled into my bed. A song by Bread came on… *"I would give everything I own… give up my life, my heart, my home… I would give everything I own… just to have you… back again."*

I cried myself to sleep. The next morning, I awoke to the smell of bacon coming from the kitchen. I thought to myself, *"Wow! It was all a dream!!"* I ran downstairs, expecting to see my mom in the kitchen, and was so happy! But as I approached the kitchen, I could see it was my grandma at the stove. "Oh," I mumbled, when she told me good morning. "It's just you."

Jeff and Chris got up soon after, and then the Bees. Neil arrived later and our house was full of people. My grandmother had to go make arrangements for the funeral. The next few days passed in a blur; then, my father arrived. His presence created an awkward situation for everyone. I had only seen him once since he had gotten out of jail.

On May 1, 1974, my mother was laid to rest. I did not shed a tear at the funeral, even when I walked up to the casket with Jeff and Christina, who were both a wreck. I reached out and touched her hand. It was so cold. Then I kissed her cheek. As I did so, I thought about how she didn't feel or smell like my mom. It was a unsettling and a little frightening. I was 13 years old, and had never seen a dead person before.

Jeff, Chris, and I took the rest of the week off from school. My father and grandmother battled over who would get to raise us. In the past few days, I had begun to get a sense of just how volatile my dad could be. Still, the court awarded custody to him, and he wanted us in Trenton as soon as possible—but only Chris, Jeff and me, not the Bees.

I didn't want to go to Trenton. I did not want to be taken away from the Bees or leave my friends. My old baseball coach, Jack Zoulek, offered to take us in and let us finish the school year in East Jordan, but my dad said no. He said he wanted us to meet some Trenton kids before school let out so we would have friends for the summer there. My buddy Versile and I swapped football jerseys so we would always remember each other.

On May 10, I said goodbye to my friends, my home in northern Michigan, and, with great sadness, the Bees. They were going to go live with Neil. I was going to live with my father—a man I barely knew—and his wife. I was heartbroken. Our lives were totally turned upside down. Again.

CHAPTER 6

Trenton

After we moved in with my dad, he and Kathy got us haircuts and took us shopping for new clothes. My mother had really neglected us in that department. When we first arrived in Trenton, we had long shaggy hair and dirty clothes that didn't properly fit. But now we looked like totally different people—like normal kids.

Even though it was the tail end of the school year, we enrolled and attended and quickly made new friends. I even had a girlfriend!

Up north, girls never noticed me. In East Jordan, there were fewer than 1,000 kids in the entire school system. Here, there were easily 500 in middle school alone, probably another 2,000 in high school.

Kathy ended up becoming an important person in my life. She was only in her mid-twenties when we moved in with her and my dad. Imagine being only 24 years old, and suddenly becoming responsible for a 14-, 13- and 11-year-old. She didn't have the chance to plan for a baby; suddenly she had teenagers who had a lot of issues. She did everything she could to make us feel comfortable and loved.

Along with having us to worry about, Kathy also had to try to manage my father, whose ideas of how to raise children were very different from hers. But she met the responsibilities head on.

She woke up early every morning and cleaned the condo. We quickly became accustomed to hearing the sound of her running the vacuum. She made up a "real" breakfast for us every morning— not cold cereal, but bacon and eggs. She packed our lunches for school every day and cooked dinner every night. She did our laundry and put it on our beds, all folded and ready to be put away. The dishes were done after every meal, and there was always food in the house. She helped us with our homework whenever we needed it. She offered great advice, and she listened. On top of everything else, she worked a full-time job.

Despite her inexperience and young age, Kathy was the picture of a mother, and I quickly grew to love and trust her. This caused a lot of friction with my dad. Many times, in a drunken rage, he would accuse her of trying to steal my affection from him. The truth is, she was the best example of a parent that I ever had. She took a lot of grief for standing up for us kids when she thought my father was being a bully or abusive.

Kathy's parents, whom we called Grandpa Joe and Grandma M, were wonderful people. They accepted Jeff, Chris, and me as their grandchildren, even though we were not related by blood. They cared for us during the summer, when my dad and Kathy were at work. I loved being at their house. There was a pool to swim in, which was great, but mostly I just loved the way they made us feel at home… wanted and loved. Grandma M. would make us lunch and always take the time to listen and talk to us.

My maternal grandmother, Eunice, was also an amazing woman. She worked very hard, both outside the home and in raising her seven children. She was a great inspiration to me; I never wanted to disappoint her.

My own mother was just a girl herself when she had us. She just wasn't equipped to raise children, especially alone. I know that she did the best she could, and I love her and miss her every day of my life.

That summer, Jeff and I helped my dad remodel the basement. We lived in a two-bedroom condo, and really needed the extra living space. We decided to put in another bedroom, a laundry room, and bar. We made a floor plan and measured everything off. We calculated out how much lumber we needed for the first phase. Dad was drinking beer while he worked, and listening to Tiger baseball on the radio.

The next morning, a Saturday, we went to the lumberyard—N.A. Mans & Sons, the same place Jeff and I had vandalized with our buddies when we were young. Even though we hadn't actually broken the windows, I still felt bad, especially because the owner's son, Nick, was now my friend.

We brought a bunch of 2x4s home and went to work applying them to the floor and ceiling. We worked all day, breaking only for lunch and dinner. After dinner, we went back to work again.

My dad had started drinking around lunchtime, so by that evening, he was pretty sauced up. After working for a while, he took a break and went upstairs. After about 10 minutes or so, we could hear him arguing with Kathy.

Jeff and I went upstairs to see what was going on. Chris was in the living room, where my dad was still yelling at Kathy. Then he suddenly punched the door. The door jam came flying across the living room, and we all ducked to avoid getting hit.

Kathy had been cleaning the bathroom, and when my dad wanted to use it, she asked him to wait a minute. He came unglued.

Later, at dinner, my dad was being very obnoxious, and Kathy didn't like it. After we finished eating, I realized just how much he disrespected her: He lit a cigarette and used his plate for an ashtray, expecting her to clean it up.

After the door-punching incident, us kids knew we needed to be on our best behavior. We didn't want to do anything that would set him off again. Don't make a wrong move or say the wrong thing, or it could lead to a disaster. It's funny how quickly you catch on to things.

The next morning, we woke up and started working again, as if nothing had happened. I guess my dad and Kathy had patched things up, because he only had a few beers that day.

Kathy always did what she could to hold things together, and deflect the attention from us to her when needed. She would usually pay the price for it, and she could only do so much. She and my dad had a new baby, Mark, so she had many more responsibilities now. Kathy was such a good mother... to all of us. She did everything she could to protect us and make a good home for us.

With the framing done, we put up paneling and began looking for carpeting the following weekend. One thing about my dad—when he got started on a project, he worked hard and fast, with the expertise of a seasoned carpenter. Within a month, we had our bedroom fully equipped, and a bar fully supplied. There was even a "kegerator." I wasn't sure if that was a blessing or a curse.

Jeff and I learned a lot from our father during those weeks of remodeling the basement. We had to develop a plan, execute that plan, put up walls, install lighting, do rewiring, lay carpet, and put in plumbing for the bar.

While we were working in the basement, my dad began telling us a little bit about his childhood. When he was 5 years old, he was sitting out in the yard playing a guitar that he had gotten for Christmas. His father came up to him and asked if he'd like a new baseball glove.

"Sure!" my dad said.

"Well give me your guitar, and I will go get you one," his father told him.

He reluctantly handed over the guitar. His father left and never came back home. A few days later, on a trip to town with his mother, he saw his guitar hanging in the window of a pawnshop.

Shortly thereafter, my dad's mother, unable to care for him, his brother, and sisters on her own, took the children to her parent's house—and left them there. My dad's siblings were eventually turned over to the state and placed into orphanages around the country. Being the youngest, he stayed with his grandparents at their farm in Huron Township.

I was stunned to realize that his parents had abandoned my father, and that he didn't see his siblings for years. It made me realize that he hadn't had the easiest childhood, either.

I felt closer to my dad that weekend than I had in a long time. He not only taught Jeff and me some valuable carpentry skills, like a good father would, he opened up to us about his past.

There were other days when my father was fun and enjoyable to be with, but they were few and far between. The problem was he drank pretty much every day. I often wonder what kind of dad he would have been without the alcohol. I think he would have been great.

I spent most of that summer in 1974 with my new Trenton friends, riding my bike to my grandmother's house in Flat Rock, or to Grandpa Joe's and Grandma M's. Jeff had other friends and was heading in a different direction than me. He was starting to become more interested in partying. I was staying out of trouble. It had been four months since we left East Jordan, and I really missed it.

I heard from old friends that Bill, my mom's old loser boyfriend, killed himself, walking into his front yard, putting his gun inside his mouth, and pulling the trigger. He was apparently despondent over the unexpected death of his stepfather, Reese.

I never really knew the real Bill or his story. Clearly, he was a troubled man. But I was just a 13-year-old boy trying to deal with all of the tragedies of my own life. I was trying to find my own way.

I can relate to the pain Bill must have felt, but I cannot understand why he gave up. No matter how dark things would get for me, I always believed they would get better, that there was a light at the end of the tunnel. "Be patient, and you will see it," I'd tell myself.

On Labor Day weekend, my dad let my grandmother take us up north so we could see the Bees and visit with our friends. Sporting a new look, Jeff, Chris, and I were going back for the first time since my mother had died. It was surreal.

Girls that never seemed to notice me before wanted to know more about me. I had a great time catching up with my close friends, Versile, Dennis, and Al. The weekend went by really fast—too fast. And before I knew it, we were on our way back to Trenton and back to school.

That year, I met a kid named Jack, and we became good friends. One day, he asked if I wanted to spend the night. As we walked home, we talked about our childhoods. The next thing you know, we were walking straight toward my old house. Then Jack said, "Yeah, when I was a little kid, a bank robber lived right next door to us!"

For a moment, I was too surprised to speak. Then I told him, "Jack, that was my dad." He stopped in his tracks and looked at me confused for a second or two and then said, 'You're David??' Neither of us had made the connection, but this was Jack Hardaway, my old friend from kindergarten.

School Picture - 1975

As we walked down the alley, my mind flashed back to the cops pulling up, and Jeff and I running in to the house in a panic. For a second, I was worried that Jack wouldn't want to be my friend anymore, now that he knew who I really was. But that wasn't the case at all.

Things at school were going great. We were eighth graders and the oldest kids in school—kind of like being seniors in high school. I played on the football team as linebacker with my friend Jimmy. I was also back-up halfback and quarterback. We were a pretty good team with a .500 record. Things at home however, were not so good.

On one hand, we had everything we needed—nice clothes, a clean house, clean clothes, and plenty of food. We had steak for dinner several times a week—it was my dad's favorite—and were all in all well provided for.

My father had a great work ethic. He was up at 6 a.m. every morning, never missed a day of work, and was one of the top mechanics at his company, which employed about 3,000 people. On the other hand, he had been becoming increasingly volatile, especially when he drank.

When I'd get home, I'd never know what I was walking into. He would get home from work at 3:30 p.m., unless he worked overtime, then it was 5:30 p.m. He worked Monday through Friday and every other weekend. On his off weekend, he would get Friday, Saturday, Sunday, and Monday off.

When he got home from work, without fail, he would go straight to the refrigerator and open a beer. After several beers, he would become obnoxious, belligerent, and downright mean. He would degrade us and call us names. He did not hesitate to cuff us upside the head if he thought we had done something wrong.

One time when we had spaghetti for supper, I started putting mine on a piece of bread, making a sandwich out of it. "What kind of trailer trash redneck are you? You don't eat that way in my house!" he barked.

Going out in public with him was flat-out embarrassing. He didn't care what he said to anybody, and you never knew when someone was going to set him off.

Life was still so much better for us though… so much better than The Dark Ages. We had a very nice Thanksgiving, and Christmas that year was great. I got a new catcher's glove and a tape recorder.

Things got much worse in 1975, though. Jeff and my dad started butting heads. My dad became very critical of both Jeff and me. It seemed neither of us could do anything right.

Jeff started running with a much faster and older crowd. In the spring, I started drinking beer with some friends. We would stand outside the 7-Eleven on King Road and wait for an old guy to walk by. Then we would ask him to buy for us. It usually took 10 or 15 minutes, but we always got our case of beer. That was eight beers apiece. I was constantly looking for reasons not to go home; the environment there was so unpleasant.

My dad coached our baseball team that year. It was a nightmare.

He always drank beer before practices and games—right in the car. "Roadies," he called them. One day at practice, Jeff was playing short-stop. During infield drills, Jeff picked up a ground ball and threw it to first base. He should have thrown it to second for a double play. My dad came unglued. *"You just cost us the game!!! Think, you dummy!!!*

Then, in front of everybody, he made Jeff run laps around the field, throwing the ball up and down saying, "I'm a dummy. I'm a dummy. I'm a dummy." the whole time.

Another time, during a game, Jeff picked up a grounder and double clutched the ball before throwing it to first. It should have been the third out, but he overthrew and the ball went over the first-baseman's head.

My dad came flying off the bench and onto the field. *"You want to play like a little girl? Then get your ass home and do the dishes!! I better not beat you home… and those dishes better be done when I get there. You better run!!"* he screamed at the top of his lungs. Jeff hustled out of there and made the mile-and-a-half trek home.

My dad got into huge arguments with the umps almost every game. I was on the receiving end of some of his tirades as well, but not as often. I didn't seem to make as many mistakes. Baseball was my game; basketball was Jeff's.

When my dad drank, he often got on this, "Yes, sir/No, sir" kick. If he asked us a question and we answered with a "Yeah," "Yes," or "Yep," it was, *"Yep? What is yep? You better answer me with respect!! You answer with me 'Yes, Sir!'"* When he wasn't drinking, we didn't have to say "sir." The trick was to figure out when you were supposed to say it, and when you weren't.

That summer, Jeff had gotten into a series of fights and other trouble. My dad thought it would be best if Jeff went to live in Indiana with our aunt, who owned a chicken farm. Dad felt that if being raised on a farm was good enough for him, it was good enough for Jeff. The hard work would do him some good. So we took Jeff to Thorntown, Ind., to meet our aunt and uncle for the first time. A few days later, my dad and I returned home to Trenton.

Jeff seemed to do well in Indiana. He played junior varsity basketball as a freshman, which was outstanding. I, on the other hand, was left with "Fireball." That's the nickname Jeff gave our dad.

It was time for the Burch family reunion, so we loaded up the car and away we went. Fireball had too much to drink before we even arrived. He started picking fights with various family members. During a softball game, other male family members had had enough of my dad's mouth, and punches were thrown. After that, we got in the car and left. This would be a recurring theme for just about every family event going forward; they always ended in a fight... a physical confrontation.

When I first moved to Trenton, I was 4 ft.-7 in. and 85 pounds. By the start of my freshman year, I was 5-ft.-7 in. and 155 pounds. Over the course of about 16 months, I had grown a foot taller and added 80 pounds. But I wasn't fat. For the first time in many years, I was nourished.

Football practice started and I was looking forward to my first year of high school. We were a really good freshman team. We played on Saturday mornings. Things were going well; I was getting a lot more playing time than I expected. I was moved to cornerback for the first two games and really liked the position.

One Thursday after practice, I went home for dinner. My dad and Kathy were into it already. I went downstairs to get away from the arguing, and heard my dad hit Kathy. This was not uncommon when they fought.

A few minutes later, Fireball came storming down the stairs. "Pack your stuff. We're gettin' outta here." It was one of his four-day weekends, so he didn't have to be back at work until the following Tuesday.

It was only about 6 p.m., but he was already pretty drunk. I did as I was told, and we got into the car. Fireball, Chris, and I were all headed to Indiana, to my aunt's house. Of course he had several beers for the ride. 'Roadies."

Chris and I fell asleep, and we got to Thorntown around 1 a.m.

It was really good to see Jeff again. He looked happy and seemed to have straightened out a lot. Unfortunately, I missed football practice on Friday and the game on Saturday. We went back home on Sunday, and Fireball acted like nothing had ever happened.

Well nothing had happened—to him at least. I lost my position on the football team and played very little after that. When you don't show up for a practice and a game, the coaches will find someone who will.

I did not play basketball that year. Instead, I went to parties on the weekends. I was really starting to lose my way... and my mind. I needed out of the house.

There was an event at the high school called "All-stars." It was like a musical play. It sounded interesting, but freshmen boys had never made it through tryouts before. Three older girls—they were juniors—asked my friend Kirk and me if we wanted to try out with them. I guess they had seen us perform in our eighth grade talent show last year and wanted us to be in their group.

Umm... hello? Of course we would do it! These girls were beautiful, and they were older! We'd have to be crazy to say no.

Kirk and I spent hours practicing, which was a nice distraction from everything else going on in my life. Eventually, we were selected to be in the show. The first freshman boys ever! It was the highlight of my whole freshman year.

The girl who had the lead in the show was a senior named Maryanne. She was dating the captain of the football team, but took a liking to me for some reason. She probably just thought it would be nice to help this little freshman kid find his way around. We would hang out a lot at practice, and she would make little things for me and give them to me... a bracelet and ring out of fabric, etc.

We started hanging out a little bit after practice as well. She took me to a hair stylist and changed my hairstyle. I'm sure it was all innocent fun to her, but I could not help falling for her. I wasn't used to girls—especially older girls—paying attention to me, and I totally misread her intentions. She felt so bad when she found out, and I felt bad for misunderstanding our friendship. We never really hung out much after that.

Jeff came home in the spring. That's when I started smoking cigarettes and dope and hanging out with a completely different group of friends, often at Teifer Park in Trenton. Things were so miserable at home, I didn't want to go there. I just wanted out. I wanted to escape.

I had lost interest in football, baseball, and basketball—things that used to mean so much to me. I would stay anywhere just to avoid going home. My father was drinking every single day, and I just couldn't take it anymore. I felt like I was losing my mind.

I told Jeff that I needed to get away. "I don't know how, but I am going to leave," I said.

Little did I know that before long, an opportunity would open up for me to do just that, through my old friend Jack Hardaway.

CHAPTER 7

Neil

By the end of June 1976, with school no longer a distraction, my despair deepened. I was losing my sense of who I was. I was smoking cigarettes, drinking, and using drugs—doing anything to escape. I realized, though, that the only real way to escape was to get away. The situation at home was not going to get better. All I could think about was returning to East Jordan.

My opportunity came when my friend Jack told me that his family was leaving in a few days to go on a two-week vacation. They were going to Burt Lake, not too far from East Jordan. My mind starting racing; here was my chance.

I spent the evening at home, planning. The next day I asked Jack if I could hitch a ride with him and his family to Neil's house. It was only about 20 miles off Interstate 75—practically on the way. He said he'd ask his parents.

In the meantime, I asked Kathy if it would be OK if I went up north on vacation with Jack. She said she'd talk to my dad for me and let me know. Later that night, Jack called to say that his parents had given the thumbs up. Not long after, Kathy told me my dad had agreed to let me go with the Hardaways.

I could hardly contain my excitement. I felt so smart!

We left early that Friday, the last weekend of June. I was at Neil's by mid-afternoon. It felt *so* great to be back home. Neil was surprised to see me, but welcomed me in. The Bees were getting so big—they were already 6 years old! I had a hard time telling them apart at first.

I spent a few hours talking to Neil and playing with the boys. I had told Neil that my dad said I could come visit for two weeks. We had dinner, then I left to go hang out with some of my old friends, the Carpenters.

They weren't home, so I walked downtown. On the way, a car passed by and then slammed on its brakes. The car backed up and my old buddy Versile got out.

We exchanged excited hellos, and I told him I was up for a two-week visit. He asked if I wanted to go with him to a keg party at the dam, and I did. It was great to see so many old friends. It had only been about two years since I left. At home in Trenton, it felt like a lifetime; back in East Jordan, with everyone welcoming me so warmly, it seemed like yesterday.

Neil told me to be home by 11 p.m., and I was. He worked from 9 p.m. to 6 a.m., so I knew he wouldn't be there to smell the beer on my breath. He had dropped the boys off at the sitter's, so I would have the house to myself.

On Saturday, I woke up and made my way to the beach. I was hoping to see more old friends there, and I wasn't disappointed. At lunch time, we headed over to the Dairy Freeze. Kathy had given me $100 before I left, which in 1976 was a lot of money. It was great to have spending money for a change. What a difference from when I used to fiddle with that quarter, standing in line at school for the free lunch.

I knew I had to be careful with the $100. It had to last—because I had no intention of ever returning to Trenton.

I spent the next few days with friends, swimming and hanging out at the beach during the day, watching softball games and going to the drive-in movie theater at night. I knew I'd eventually have to talk with Neil, but I wasn't ready to do so quite yet. I had told the Hardaways that my aunt was going to drive me back to Trenton, so they wouldn't come back to East Jordan to pick me up on their way home.

The Fourth of July weekend was magical. There was a carnival in town, and the population of the town seemed to double. A lot of people from "down state" and around Chicago have summer homes in northern Michigan. The locals call the tourists "fudgies," because of the area fudge shops they frequent.

That summer, as always, there were fudgies everywhere. I guess I was one of them! Funny thing is, I didn't feel like it. I felt like East Jordan was where I belonged.

I was dreading the talk with Neil, and kept putting it off, but he beat me to the punch. I had spent the day at the beach, and he was waiting for me out front when I got home. I could tell something was up, and tried to think fast.

"Did your dad give you permission to come here?" he asked.

"Not exactly," I admitted.

"What do you mean by that?" he said.

I told him that my dad had agreed to let me go to Burt Lake with my friend and his family... I just altered the plans a bit. He told me to go on, and I admitted that my dad didn't know I was in East Jordan at all.

Neil then said that my dad must have figured things out, because he called and told Neil to have me back in Trenton within 24 hours, or he'd have him put in jail for kidnapping.

I looked at Neil and knew that I'd only have one chance to sell him on the idea I had been keeping inside. I went into sales mode.

"Neil, you have two 6-year-old boys and you work the third shift. I'm guessing you spend at least $100 a week on a babysitter. Plus, you have to clean the house and take care of the Bees during the day when you should be sleeping."

"And??" was his reply.

"I can change all that," I said. "I can be home at 9 o'clock every night to watch the Bees. And when they go to bed, I can do the dishes and clean the house. You can save $400 every month, and have a clean house—and I can get out of my dad's house."

I told him that I was 15 years old and could petition the court to decide where I live. I told him that I could convince a judge to let me stay.

He didn't answer yes or no. He just said, "I told your dad you'd call him when you got back."

It was at that moment I realized that we were standing in the exact spot we had been when Neil told me my mom had died.

I reluctantly went inside the house and called Fireball. I could tell he was about six or seven beers into his evening, and that it would not be a pleasant conversation. He started by telling me what an ungrateful little brat I was, and that I had better be home within 24 hours.

I told him that I was not coming back, that my home was in East Jordan and not with him.

"Because I threw some garbage in your bed?! You're gonna hold that against me?" he yelled.

I said, "No, dad. It's not because of the garbage."

I told him that he was out of control and that I needed to do this for me. "It's not about you, Dad," I said.

He hung up the phone... and that was that.

I told Neil what had happened, and asked if I could stay. He agreed.

The next day, we went to the county courthouse to get the process started. We were given a trial date in August. Assuming that we'd win, Neil went ahead and enrolled me in school.

I spent the rest of the summer hanging out with my old friends, and new ones I had met at the beach. There was a group of kids, mostly girls, there every day. They were a couple of years younger than me, but fun to be around. Most of my friends my own age had jobs during the day, but I didn't, as my job was to watch the boys at night. In the evening, we would go to the softball games and hang out, but I never missed my 9 p.m. curfew.

It was that summer that I met Joan. She had very blond hair, blue eyes, an athletic shape, and was very shy. I fell head over heels in love with her. There was just something special about her. She was only going into the eighth grade though, and I felt guilty about my feelings toward her. I was 15 years old and going into tenth grade. She was not yet 13. I knew it couldn't work, and I valued our friendship too much to push it.

One day in August, I was at the morning session of a two-a-day junior varsity football practice, and Coach Gee came up to me and told me that Neil was here to see me. I was in the hurdler stretch position, and happy to get up and take a break. I knew Neil had gone to the Charlevoix County Courthouse for our trial, and I was eager to hear how it had turned out.

Neil told me that my dad hadn't shown up for court, and that the judge had awarded custody of me to Neil. I was so happy! *"Thank you, Neil. Thank you! Thank you!"*

I was free. Everything worked out just the way I wanted it to. Later that evening, though, it occurred to me that I had been abandoned yet again. My dad didn't even show up; he didn't try to fight for me. I wanted to live with Neil, and I was the one who left Trenton, but it still stung that he didn't care enough to want me back.

If it were my son, I would walk through the fires of hell to get him back... to love him and protect him and show him I cared. But my dad did not. It was a relief to know I could stay in East Jordan, but I felt very alone.

I knew that my relationship with Neil was one of convenience. He needed me, I needed him. I knew going in not to expect hugs and kisses or expressions of affection. It was a business transaction. I accepted the situation for what it was, and knew this would be the way it would go for the next three years or so.

As time went on, however, we did, in fact, form a special bond— the closest thing to a father-son relationship I had ever known. I have to admit, though, I didn't always make it easy for him.

I kept up with my responsibilities around the house. I had to be home by 9 p.m., Sunday through Thursday. I was expected to do the dishes, laundry, and light cleaning around the house, in addition to taking care of the twins. We had a woodstove, so I needed to fill it with wood before bed, and wake up at 5 a.m. to refill it again, so the house would be warm when we got up for school.

After my mom died, Neil quit smoking and drinking and started going to church. One of the conditions of me living with him was that I had to attend as well. This was OK with me. I was no longer angry at God, and I was ready to make amends.

The only time I could work outside the home to make some spending money was on the weekends and in the summer during the day. I got a job at The Country House, a restaurant and bar owned by close family friends, Mary and Ed Brzozowy. I worked there as a short-order cook on Fridays and Saturdays from 5 p.m. to midnight.

In the summer, I landed a job at a farm called Dad's Clearing, in a rural area south of town. If you've never hauled hay, let me tell you, it is *hard* work, and it made for very long days. You'd work for a week or two, and then have a week or two off. The pay was good for a high school kid, though. I really didn't have a lot of choices when it came to a job, due to my other commitments.

Sometime in early August, just before football practices started up again, Jeff showed up in East Jordan, wanting to move in with Neil and me. He had been staying with my aunt for the past year or so, but wanted to be back up north.

Things went well for the first seven or eight months. Jeff and

I would alternate days to watch the Bees. We both played football and basketball, and all was well. We walked to school because the bus stopped at our house around 7 a.m., and Neil wasn't quite back from work yet. As we couldn't leave the twins alone, we walked the 2 or 3 miles to school instead.

On one of those walks in late March, Jeff said to me, "Dave, if anyone asks where I am today, just tell them you don't know."

"Why? What are you doing?" I asked

"I'm hitchhiking to the Hash Bash," he said.

"What the heck is that?" I asked.

Jeff explained that on the first Saturday of April, a bunch of people gather in Ann Arbor to celebrate the lax marijuana laws in the city, and just get high all weekend.

I couldn't believe that he was going to hitchhike all the way to Ann Arbor—about 150 miles away—just to get high with others.

Sure enough, about mid-morning, I got called in to the office. Neil was there, and he and the principal asked me if I knew where Jeff was. I told them that the last I knew, Jeff was at school. I felt really bad about not being truthful with them, but I couldn't rat out my brother. Fireball always told us, "No one likes a snitch."

I would never lie to Neil again.

Jeff got back on Monday, and Neil warned Jeff that he better straighten up and fly right from then on. Things remained a bit rocky between them, then in August, Jeff went to the Cherry Festival in Traverse City with friends. He must have drank a lot, because when Neil came home, he found Jeff sleeping on the front porch holding a stuffed animal he had won at the fair. I woke up to them yelling at each other. It was the last straw, and Neil asked Jeff to move out. Within a week, he was gone, bunking instead with some friends.

I had a great year in sports that year. I had quit smoking pot and cut way back on smoking cigarettes and drinking beer. I tried and tried to quit smoking cigarettes altogether, but couldn't quite kick it. I was asked to move up to the varsity football team with Versile and another player, but decided to stay on junior varsity with Coach Gee, because of my respect for him, and because I knew I'd get more playing time.

In the spring, I made the varsity baseball team as the starting catcher. I had to beat out some good athletes to win the job. I also was at the top of the batting order and feeling quite proud about that.

I started hanging out with Sherri and Jackie, the daughters of my boss at The Country House, Mr. Brzozowy. The family was from Trenton, originally, and had been friends with my mother when she lived there. What a small world that both of our families would end up in this tiny northern Michigan town.

My gym teacher was a man named Mr. Burrows. He was a strong teacher and demanded perfection, the kind he learned in the military. In class, we had to stand in formation, and we had inspection. He taught us how to march and a lot about discipline.

Some kids did not like his class because he was strict, but I thought he did a great job teaching us about accountability. I learned a lot about life from Mr. Burrows, and have a great respect for him to this day.

The girls from the beach, Joan and her friend Pat, asked me to coach their summer league softball team. I agreed to do it, because it sounded like fun. Luckily, it was all for fun, because the team did not win many games. I focused on teaching them the fundamentals and knew in time they'd do well.

That summer, Joan and Pat and I became very close. We would spend days at the beach, evenings at the softball field, and nights on the phone. I would talk to Joan three or four times a week while I was watching the boys. To her, we were just friends. But I had much deeper feelings for her—and had from the very first moment we met.

I also talked to Pat on the phone several nights a week. Mostly I talked to her about Joan. Pat was the one who let me know that Joan did not like me as a boyfriend, just as a really good friend. I accepted that; I had no choice.

Joan was the all-American girl, and I was a guy with a tortured past. She would always have my heart, though, and that wasn't a big secret among the people who knew us. One night, I went to the county fair with my friends Doug, Bob, and Shirley. I only had a little money to spend; instead of using it to ride a ride or play a game, I spent all of it on a bracelet for Joan. It was a leather strap that I had her name embossed on. I gave it to her the next day, and she really seemed to like it.

At the end of summer, I stopped working at The Country House, but would spend Friday and Saturday evenings at Sherri and Jackie's house. As their parents worked late at the bar, we were unsupervised. A group of our friends would play cards and board games and just hang out. We were all quite close.

During the fall, I started a relationship with a girl. Being young and naïve, things became intimate way before I was ready. It was my first experience in that department, and it became complicated very quickly. The next thing I knew, she told me that she had missed her period.

Suddenly, it hit me. I never intended to make the same mistakes my parents had made, but here I was, facing a teenage pregnancy. It scared the crap out of me. But mostly, I was disappointed in myself... for not having more self-control... for showing such little respect for my girlfriend... for heading down the same path as my father.

CHAPTER 8

Joan

Much to our relief, it turned out to be a false alarm.

But our relationship would never be the same, and we broke up soon after. I'm grateful that we became good friends, however, and remain so to this day.

After the pregnancy scare, I made a commitment to myself to abstain from sex, at least until I got married and could afford to support my wife and child. At the time, I couldn't even afford to support myself.

The school year ended and I spent another summer working in the hay fields, and working at The Country House on Friday and Saturday nights. On my days off, I would hang out at the beach with Joan and her friends. I also coached their softball team again.

The beach always brought me great joy. It was a place where my friends and I could be ourselves, without parents or teachers around. It was just us kids hanging out, swimming, soaking up the sun, and talking about life and our dreams for the future.

My dream was to play baseball at the highest level I could— maybe even professionally. Baseball just came naturally for me, and I worked hard to develop my skills.

That summer, my feelings for Joan were to the point of outright love—deep, deep love. By now, she had become a young woman... more beautiful than ever. Don't get me wrong; I'm not so shallow as to fall in love with a girl just because of the way she looks.

Joan had gorgeous blue eyes, pure blonde hair that would make Marilyn Monroe jealous, a smile that was better than Farrah Fawcett's and a body most girls could only wish for. But forget all that. She was the most loving, caring person I knew. Loyal to the end, she would do anything to help someone in need. She always cared about how I was doing and what was going on in my life.

She was also driven to succeed in life and did everything 100 percent, and was just as competitive as me. We spent a lot of time together at the beach and had long conversations on the phone. Although she didn't have the same romantic feelings for me, I was still madly in love with her. I would date several girls before I graduated from high school, but Joan was the only one who truly had my heart.

One day while we were at the beach, I asked Joan to walk to the Dairy Freeze with me. She said, "Sure, if you're going to buy me a banana split!" She was the only person I knew who loved banana splits, but ordered them without the bananas—or whipped cream, or nuts.

As we walked, we talked about the Detroit Tigers and what they needed to do to make a run for the pennant. That's another thing I loved about Joan. She adored the Tigers and loved to talk about baseball.

When we got to the Dairy Freeze, I ordered two banana splits, and Joan quickly said, "No. I was just kidding! You don't have to buy me a banana split." I compromised and changed the order to one for us to share—no bananas, no whipped cream, no nuts.

We sat at the picnic table and enjoyed our treat and each other's company. I asked her if she'd like to go to my house, which was nearby, to get my radio so we could listen to the Tigers game at the beach. She said yes, and we walked, talking all the while.

Once at my house, Joan sat on the couch near the stereo, and I went upstairs to find my transistor. While looking for it, I noticed an album that I played many nights before I went to sleep. It had a song on it that always made me think of Joan. I picked up the album along with the radio and headed back downstairs. I asked Joan if I could play a song for her and she agreed. The song was "To Love Somebody" by the Bee Gees. The lyrics tell the story of a man who's in love with a woman who does not feel the same way.

I asked her to dance, and as we swayed to the music, I sang softly in her ear, "You don't know what it's like… to love somebody, to love somebody the way I love you.." It was a very bold move for me, but I had to do it. When the song ended, she hugged me, kissed me on the cheek and said thank you.

We didn't say a whole lot on the walk back to the beach… both deep in thought. Just before we reached the beach, Joan grabbed my hand and we walked over to a picnic table.

"Wow! The song worked!!" I thought.

We sat down next to each other and she began to talk. I could tell that she was very nervous. She told me that she was sorry if she gave me the wrong impression about our relationship. She told me she had feelings for me, but as a friend... that she valued our friendship very deeply, but that was all it could be right now.

I told her I knew that, which is why I played the song for her. "It's OK, Joan," I said. "That song is us right now. But someday, I will ask you to marry me. You will say yes, and we will live happily ever after." I told her my feelings for her would never change.

Joan, East Jordan High School

When we got back to the beach, our friends asked where we had been for so long. All of them knew of my feelings for Joan, and I think some of them thought maybe we were finally a couple. No such luck.

Over the rest of the summer, I began making a David and Joan song list. One of the songs was "Love Will Find a Way" by Pablo Cruise. Another was "Still the One" by Orleans. Both bands were coming to Castle Farms, an area concert venue, in a few weeks so I saved my money and bought two tickets to the show. My friend Duane and I were going to double-date. When I asked Joan, she informed me that her father would never let her go out on a date, much less to a concert. She was still just 14 years old. I was disappointed, but not defeated. I told her that I'd be thinking of her.

The girls' softball team finished just under .500 that year. The team was getting better and I knew that by the following year, we'd have a shot at winning the league.

Summer was winding down, and I was excited to start my senior year of high school. I had an old 1968 Ford pickup to drive, which was nice. It had a "three on the tree," which means it was a three-speed, with the shifter on the steering wheel column. The only problem was, occasionally the shifter fell off, as it was attached only by a hose clamp. Whenever it did so, I'd jam a Phillip's screwdriver I kept on the seat into the socket to use as a shifter until I could get somewhere to properly reattach it.

One afternoon, I was heading to Boswell Field to watch the junior varsity football game. I spotted Joan and a friend walking. Joan was wearing her cheerleading uniform, which she looked extra hot in. I pulled over and offered a ride. Joan jumped in next to me, and her friend beside her. As I started driving, we were talking and laughing. I shifted into second, and sure enough—off comes the shifter. Joan's eyes almost popped out of her head as she looked at it dangling in my hand. I said, "I need the screwdriver!"

The girls frantically looked around, but could not find it. I reached under Joan's butt and grabbed the screwdriver. She shrieked as I did.

"Wow!" she exclaimed. "What a set-up."

I just laughed, realizing nothing I could say would make her think otherwise.

Our varsity football team was on fire; we ended up going 8-1 for the season and beat rival Mancelona for the first time in 20 years.

After football practice – 1978

Still, it was a bit of a disappointment for me, as I did not play as much as I would have liked. One day, after the season was over, Duane and I were walking from the parking lot into school when one of the assistant coaches called us over to his car. He told me he was really sorry that I didn't play more, but that it was out of his hands.

I said, "You're the coach, how could it be out of your hands?" He told me, "Let's just say that there was a certain parent-coach who had a different agenda."

That year, I learned about politics in high school sports, as well as politics in life in general. I was shown that sometimes, it's not what you can do—it's about your last name.

I never had the right last name. I remember thinking how unfair it was that I couldn't have been born into the right family. I also remember thinking how selfish it was for one self-centered parent to ruin it for other kids. It was all about his kid and his kid's friends, not about what was best for the team. This is a theme I've seen over and over in high school sports.

At the end of football season, we got a new principal. He was supposedly brought in to restore discipline, although none of the students seemed to think such a problem existed. One day, I was late for lunch, as I had to finish up some work for class. I got my food and sat down with my friends. As they were already finished eating, I told them to go ahead and I'd catch up with them later. Several of them had left their milk cartons and other trash scattered around on the table. The new principal walked up and said, "David, I trust that you are going to pick up this mess before you leave?" I replied, "No sir, it is not mine. I have my trash right here and I will take care of that."

"Well I would assume that this trash is from your friends, so pick it up or meet me in my office after lunch," he said.

There were many milk cartons and other trash on the tables, not just in our area and not just from my friends. So I finished my lunch, walked directly to his office, and waited for him. When he arrived, he asked why I didn't pick up the trash. I told him, "I'm a student, not a janitor." He suspended me for three days.

I guess he was trying to make an example out of me. It felt like he thought I was insignificant and not upstanding enough—another example of having the wrong last name. This would never happen to the son of one of the more prominent families in the community. I could have just picked up the trash and been done with it, but I couldn't. I felt I had to stand up for myself.

I walked home, and when I got there, Neil wanted to know why I wasn't in school. I told him what happened. Surprisingly, Neil took me back to school and, after giving the principal a piece of his mind, I was able to return to class. It felt really good to have someone go to bat for me.

Unfortunately, the new principal would have the last laugh. During Christmas break we had basketball practice. I was having a good season up to that point. After practice, I saw one of my friends walking with a large clear plastic bag full of cans. I caught up to him and as we walked together. I asked where he got all of the cans.

"The teachers' lounge" he replied. I laughed and said, "Man, you have to take those back! Don't you think they will notice that they are missing?" He said he didn't care. I walked with him to Glen's Market, a local grocery store, where he turned in the cans and received about $20. (Michigan has a 10-cent deposit program for bottles and cans; so each empty is worth a dime.) As we left, I told him he should return the money to the school—and tried to convince him to do so several times during the break—but he refused.

On the Monday morning that we went back to school, the guilt sunk in. He agreed that he should have turned the money in, but he had already spent it. He said he'd talk to the principal and admit what he had done. I told him that I would loan him the money to make the repayment, and everything would be okay. As we walked in to school, the principal met us in the hallway. "Just the two I need to see. Come with me"

Once we were in his office, he asked for an explanation. My friend admitted everything and said, "Dave had nothing to do with it." He tried to give him the $20 that I had loaned him and said that he was very sorry. The principal suspended us both and kicked us off the basketball team. I was so angry. My friend came from a poorer family, just like me. Yes, he had done something wrong, but he tried to make amends. I did nothing wrong—yet we were both punished. It seemed so unfair.

Later, another friend and I were in charge of emptying the money out of the teacher's lounge pop machine. Some of the money came up missing and I was automatically accused of stealing it. This friend's father was a very prominent member of the community, on the police force. Of course it wasn't him... it had to be me. Again I was called in to the office and blamed. Luckily, the friend came forward and told the truth, and he was believed.

Sometimes things are going to happen to you that are unjust. But you can't let them bring you down. You have to rise above it and turn the other cheek.

At the beginning of my senior year, Joan and I had our first class together: Typing I. I sat right in front of her. One of my favorite things to do was to toss a wadded-up ball of paper into her machine during a timed typing test, which would jam up the machine. She used to get so mad at me for doing that!

Later, we had study hall together. This was the best part of my whole day. She told me that she took the class to get some homework done, but nobody did any studying. Again, I sat in front of her. When she wore her cheerleading uniform, I used to touch her leg and make her giggle. The teacher would see and say, "David, get your hands off Joan." My favorite comeback line was, "But my mother always told me my hands would look better on a woman."

On my birthday, I told Joan that she didn't have to give me a present, I only wanted a kiss. "Not here," she said. "OK," I replied. "But every day that goes by, I am adding one more kiss on." She giggled and blushed.

One day in class, I was looking at a *Sports Illustrated* magazine and came across an ad for a jewelry store featuring a big diamond ring. I carefully tore it out and turned around and said to Joan, "Do you remember when I told you that I was going to marry you?" Joan has many different smiles; she gave me her nervous one. I explained that without a ring, we are not truly engaged, and that I had looked and looked and finally found the right one.

She didn't know what I was doing and looked very nervous. I handed her the picture of the ring and said, "There. We are properly engaged." Out came her "something's funny" smile, and she started laughing. I could see her beautiful face turn red, but she looked happy. It was as though her feelings for me were changing, at least in my mind.

I started working out every day, as baseball season was not far off. I really wanted to do well my last year of high school. A baseball scholarship was the only hope I had of going to college. I had an OK football season, basketball was a complete disaster, so baseball was my last chance. I had been running, lifting weights, put on 10 pounds, and was in the best shape of my life. I was doing well in practice. I was hitting well and my arm was strong. I hoped to become an All-State catcher.

The day before our first game, I was catching while the team took batting practice. My friend Al was pitching, throwing mostly fastballs. What happened next changed everything. A kid named Tommy came up to bat. Al threw one of his famous fastballs. Tommy took a cut at it, and foul-tipped the ball right onto the top of the middle finger of my throwing hand. It felt like someone hit it with a hammer.

I dropped my glove, grabbed my hand and ran to a small pile

of remaining snow, where I plunged my hand in it. The coach came to look at it and asked me how I felt. My finger was throbbing and swelling up, but I told him to just give me a minute and I would be fine. I finished catching the team's batting practice, but didn't take my turn at hitting.

Later that night as I was home watching the Bees, my finger was on fire. The throbbing pain was so intense I could barely stand it. I could not go to the ER, so I called my friend Duane. He came over and when he saw my finger he told me that he thought it was broken. He told me that his dad or uncle or cousin or somebody had this same thing happen to him, and when he went to the ER, all they did was drill a hole in the nail to let the blood out. "Once the pressure is gone, you will feel so much better." "OK," I hesitantly said. "So what do we do?"

"Well, we have two options. Drill it, or heat up the end of a hanger until it's red hot. That will melt your nail and let the blood out." Neither option sounded appealing. We used a glass of ice water to numb my finger. Duane heated up a coat hanger and stuck it right in the middle of my fingernail. It was at that point that I realized that ice was not an anesthetic. It hurt so bad! I took it as long as I could, and when Duane pulled the hanger away, there was a pretty good-sized hole. But it wasn't deep enough to let the blood out. I told him I couldn't bear to repeat the process.

He went in the garage and got a 1/8-inch drill bit. After heating that up, he put it in the hole and started turning it. It did not take long before he stuck gold. Blood spurted out like oil out of a well. We put peroxide, rubbing alcohol, and a bandage on it, and it felt much better. The next day, though, my finger was throbbing again, so I went to the health clinic. When the doctor found out what we did, he said, *"What the heck were you thinking?!* My finger was fractured in three places.

I would only play as catcher in six out of 23 regular games and six out of 12 conference games that year. The first game back was against Inland Lakes. I threw out six of six runners trying to steal. The Inland Lakes coach had previously scouted our team, when I wasn't playing, and apparently thought it was OK to allow his players to steal. Afterward, he came up and congratulated me on a good game. When he asked why I hadn't been playing before, I explained what had happened.

I got All-Conference Honorable Mention, which I should have been grateful for, considering how little I played. But I was extremely disappointed. My whole senior year was a disappointment athletically. I would not get a baseball scholarship; college was out of the question.

CHAPTER 9

Cherry Blast

I graduated from high school and started looking for work. 1979 in the United States, particularly in Michigan, was a dismal time to be doing so. Unemployment was at 11 percent, and there were no available jobs in East Jordan. After the Fourth of July weekend, my brother and I packed up and moved to my grandmother's house near Detroit. I applied for work at GM, Ford, Chrysler, AMC, DTE Energy, etc., without any luck.

Jeff had been recruited to play basketball at several colleges. He decided to go with Grand Rapids Junior College. It was on the other side of the state, but at least it was in Michigan. By August, I still hadn't found a job. Jeff and I drove to Grand Rapids and got him enrolled in school, then picked up Chris from our grandma's and headed to East Jordan for the Labor Day holiday. For the three of us, it was our last weekend together as a family.

On Sunday, Jeff headed off to school and Chris went home. I stayed in East Jordan, and three days later, I managed to get a job at the Holiday gas station in nearby Charlevoix. I worked for $3 an hour, Monday through Friday, 7 a.m. to 2 p.m. I bought a 1974 Vega, and that was my ride.

Duane was in his senior year at school; we were still best friends. I went to every football game. Joan was a junior and a cheerleader. We were still very good friends as well.

Neil and Duane's mom, Barb, had been dating and were planning on getting married at Christmas time. Barb took over watching the Bees at night, so I was no longer needed there.

That fall, I started dating a girl named Heather. I would go to work every day and pick her up after school. I'd take her home and would spend the evenings with her and her family. Her father and I grew to become close. He had served in the Army in Korea in the late 1950s, and when he came home, he married his wife. He told me that the best thing he ever did for himself was join the Army.

After he got out of the service, he started working for a medical company and was doing very well.

In late November, when it was about 15 degrees and I was outside pumping gas—this was before self-service was available—I realized that there had to be something better in life. That afternoon, I picked up Heather, as usual, and we went to her house. I asked her dad how someone would go about joining the Army. He told me what needed to be done, and the next day I went to see a recruiter.

My life was going nowhere. I was drinking every night after I left Heather's house. I'd stop by to see some friends who lived in a trailer, and we'd play cards and drink beer, sometimes as late as 2 a.m. Then I'd drag myself out of bed a few hours later to get to my minimum-wage job.

Heather's dad told me that some of the Army posts had semi-professional baseball teams, and that if I was good enough, I could play there. I asked the recruiter if this was true and he said yes, although he couldn't guarantee that I'd get to a post that had a baseball team. A Sergeant sitting behind him told him that he just came from Fort Bragg, N.C., and there was a baseball team there.

"What do I have to do to go to Fort Bragg?" I asked.

"Jump out of planes," said the Sergeant.

"Like a paratrooper?" I said. "I can do that"

Before I knew it, I was on a plane headed to Detroit to get enlisted in the Army. I enrolled in the delayed entry program and was scheduled to leave for Fort Jackson, S.C., on January 22, 1980. Flying back to East Jordan after the enlistment, I started to wonder what I had just done.

Jeff supported my decision, and so did Heather's dad. He told me, "You may not think so right now, but you will not regret your decision."

During that in-between time, I continued the same cycle of working, hanging out at Heather's house, and partying. When it came time to leave, Neil and I had a heart-to-heart. I thanked him for allowing me to stay with him. He told me that my mother would be proud of my decision, and that he was also proud of me. He thanked me for all of my help during the past few years. This meant a lot to me, as Neil rarely showed affection toward me.

I packed a brown grocery bag full of clothes. I had never owned a suitcase in my life, so the bag would have to do.

"What is that?" Neil asked.

"My clothes" I said.

He laughed and said, "You're not going to need those. You're going to be wearing nothing but green for the next eight weeks! All you need is a change of underwear, a razor, and a toothbrush."

He told me to go put the clothes away. "Trust me," he said. He handed me a $10 bill and wished me good luck. "I know you will do well."

Neil had served in the 4th Mechanized Infantry division in the early 1960s, before Vietnam, and he was proud of his service. He got out as a Sergeant. My joining was bittersweet for him.

On Jan. 22, Duane and Jackie (his girlfriend, and my longtime friend) took the day off from school, with permission from their parents, and drove me to the airport, about 50 miles away. On the way there, we talked about how much fun we all had together. It was an unusually bright day, with the sun's rays reflecting off the winter snow. We stopped at McDonald's, which was a treat (there was no fast food in East Jordan; it was too small of a town).

Duane and Jackie walked into the airport with me and kept me company while I waited for the plane. These were two of my best friends, and I sure was going to miss them. When it was time to board, I reluctantly got up from my seat. Jackie gave me a hug and kiss on the cheek. Duane shook my hand. "Good luck, buddy," he said. "I'll miss you"

Once on the plane, I had time to think. I thought about Heather, and my doubts that our relationship could withstand the distance and years of separation. She was young and still in high school, and it wouldn't be fair to expect otherwise. I wondered what was in store for me at the Army base. All I could imagine was Gomer Pyle's barracks. I thought about how much my life was about to change, and whether or not I had made the right decision. I wondered if I would even make it through basic training, or if I'd fail and get kicked out. My mind was racing.

When I arrived at Detroit Metro Airport, a Sergeant was waiting for me. He took me to a processing center, where I had a physical. I was then given a folder with my orders, a plane ticket, hotel pass, and meal tickets for the Howard Johnson in downtown Detroit. This was the first time I had ever stayed in a hotel.

I was dropped off at around 5 p.m., checked into the hotel, and found my room. I thought about how I had just taken my first plane ride in November, and now I was going to be jumping out of them. I used the meal voucher and had dinner, then went for a walk. I passed a liquor store on the way and stopped in to purchase a six-pack. Back in the hotel room, I found the Piston's game on TV, but turned the volume all the way down. I liked to listen to music and watch sports on TV at the same time. I put the radio on and opened a beer.

As I opened up the packet I was given at the processing center, "Traveling Man-Beautiful Loser" by Bob Seger came on. I had adopted that as my life story song. My whole life I had moved around a lot, and I was a loser—hence, the theme. How ironic that it happened to come on now.

The very next song to play was "To Love Somebody" by the Bee Gees, the song that I had played for Joan.

I had been preparing myself for the likely breakup with Heather, and I was OK with that. But this song took me by surprise, and I lost it. I stood up and threw the folder across the room, paced back and forth a few times, then began sobbing. It had hit me all at once. My life was never going to be the same. Joan was in East Jordan, all of my good friends were there, and I was going in the Army for three years.

Joan would be a sophomore in college by the time I'd get out. She'd have a boyfriend, or maybe even be married by then, and will have forgotten all about me. What about Duane, Jackie, Tim, Sherri? All of my close friends would move on with their lives.

I suddenly realized the ramification of my decision and that nothing would ever be the same. The self-pity set in. Why couldn't I have been normal? Why couldn't I have had a real family that took care of me? My friends all had real parents who helped them get in to college to become whatever they wanted to be. I only had myself to rely on. Why did I always have to be on my own? Why did everything have to be so hard for me? I had a lot of questions… and no answers.

When I left Detroit the next morning, it was snowing and 20 degrees. We arrived in Atlanta and it was sunny and 60 degrees. I had never been out of Michigan before. "Wow!" I thought. "This is great."

I boarded the Army bus with a bunch of other recruits, people from all over the United States. On the long ride there, I saw my first palm tree. Others had Spanish moss hanging from them. I was in a different world.

Once at Fort Jackson, the bus came to a stop. We bounded off, and the fun began.

"GET MOVING YOU MAGGOTS!! I DON'T KNOW WHAT YOU MAGGOTS ARE THINKING, BUT YOU ARE MINE FOR THE NEXT EIGHT WEEKS! LET'S GOOO!!" "YOUR MOMMA AINT GONNA BE HERE TO WIPE YOUR BUTT ANYMORE! I'M YOUR MOMMA, YOUR DADDY, YOUR EVERYTHING!! THE SOONER YOU GET THAT THROUGH YOUR HEAD, THE SOONER WE'LL GET ALONG!!"

"Oh my God! What have I gotten myself in to?! I wondered.

Sgt. First Class Barnes and Staff Sgt. Ellerbe marched us to our temporary barracks to drop off our stuff, and then it was on to the mess hall. We each had 5 minutes to eat. That would hold true throughout the entire eight weeks of basic training. The Sergeants constantly reminded us, "Five minutes is plenty of time to eat—you can taste it later."

After chow, we went to supply to get our bedding for our bunks. We'd be in the temporary barracks for three days or so. At the end of the week, after processing, we'd be moved to our home for the remainder of boot camp. We were in old WWII barracks, two stories high and made of wood—the kind you see in the movies *Stripes* and *Private Benjamin*. I can't remember which, but one of those movies was actually filmed at Fort Jackson.

We spent the rest of that week getting shots, haircuts, measured for shoes, boots, clothes, and dress greens. We would also be issued our training equipment, sleeping bags, helmet, webbed gear, etc. By the end of the week, we had everything we needed. Neil was right; I wasn't going to need that brown paper sack of clothes.

On Saturday, we moved into our barracks on Tank Hill. By now, we all had a pretty good grasp on how to march, as we marched everywhere we went. (Of course I had an advantage, with all of that early training in my high school P.E. class with Mr. Burrows.)

The following Monday, I was appointed First Squad Leader.

This was a great honor. As First Squad Leader, I was the ranking member of our platoon when the Sergeants were not present. We had about 200 men and about 30 women in our training class, split up in to three platoons, each with four squads. I was the only one to hold my position as squad leader all eight weeks, while the other leaders in my platoon were replaced several times.

Although I was growing as a man and my confidence and body were getting stronger, I still struggled with homesickness, especially on Sundays, when we were given time to call home, write letters, and take care of personal matters.

During mail call, when most everyone was getting letters, cards, and care packages from home, there was rarely anything for me. Heather had written a few letters, but the end was obvious for both of us, and we decided to break up.

Finally, two letters came from Joan, which I treasured. My friend Sherri also sent me cookies and other goodies.

I usually finished first in our PT (physical training) tests and obstacle course training. I could run the mile and 2-mile quite well, and only one person in our battalion was faster. On my 19th birthday, Staff Sgt. Ellerbe and Sgt. FC Barnes were all fired up about the 1980 U.S. Olympic Men's Hockey Team. They had beaten Russia 4-3 the day before. They made the point that a bunch of young college kids from the United States had beaten the Red Army hockey team. One of them yelled out, "They kicked those commie bastards' butts!"

I considered this my birthday present, as I got no cards or cake that day.

During one day of tactical training, the Sergeants had a test for us. We were broken up into squads. There was a slab of concrete between our barracks that was about 20 ft. by 40 ft. Each team was lined up single file at opposite sides of the slab. One team was the aggressor and the other team was the defender. The aggressor had to move his men to the other side, single file without being stopped. The defender's squad had to stop the forward progress of the aggressor by getting in their way. Since I was the squad leader, it was my job to figure out a strategy and to march my squad using military commands.

The first time, my squad was the aggressor. We marched past the defenders without any trouble. The next groups of aggressors also had no problem. It seemed impossible to stop the forward progress of the aggressor. Next it was my squad's turn to be the defender. Somehow, there had to be a way to stop the other squad. I had to think fast if we were going to win this. Then an idea came to me.

We took our positions at the end of the slab and Sgt. Barnes blew his whistle. I marched my squad forward four steps, and then made a quick right turn to the edge of the slab. Then made a left, followed by another quick left and marched to the other edge of the slab. I marched my squad of about 20 men in a circle from edge to edge. Ha! The strategy worked.

Later that week, SFC Barnes called me in to his office. He said that he had never seen anyone figure out how to stop the aggressor in basic training. He said this, along with other things I had done, made him believe that I would make an excellent Officer and career soldier.

He asked if I wanted to be nominated to go to Officer's Candidate School. This was a great honor and confidence-booster for me. I thanked him and told him my first goal was to make it through basic training, and I'd set new goals once I completed that.

We were a few weeks from graduation but still had a few big challenges before we got there. First was the NBC (Nuclear Biological Chemical) gas training, which involved walking into a room filled with tear gas. If you fitted your mask properly, it was a piece of cake. They did, however, make us take the mask off briefly and breathe in the gas—not a pleasant experience.

Next was the Bivouac. For this test, we were taken out in the woods, where we would camp for a few days. During that time, we would be tested on first aid and tactical training (battle tactics and patrolling tactics). At the end of Bivouac, we would march the 25 miles back to the barracks wearing about 40 pounds worth of gear. Some guys weren't able to complete this, and that was the end of their Army career.

The next day, we were given a six-hour pass. We would have to be back in the barracks at 2300 (11 p.m.), but were free for the first time in eight weeks. We all walked to the Enlisted Members Club and I enjoyed some ice-cold beer. I didn't drink too much, as I was still responsible for the entire platoon. I was ultimately the one accountable for getting everyone back to the barracks on time—with no exceptions.

It's funny how people always want to play matchmaker. There

was a First Squad Leader in the girls' platoon who was very nice. She was an athletic, all-American girl, and my buddies thought we'd make a good couple. We danced a few times, but didn't really click. Another very attractive girl there began buying me drinks, but then I found out she was married. When the evening ended, she became angry with me because I wouldn't go to the on-post hotel with her.

At 10 p.m., I told our platoon that we had to start heading back. Many of them did, but there were a few who were talking to girls and didn't want to leave. They somehow thought that they could go to the hotel and continue to party with the girls and show up the next morning without being caught. I explained that this would not happen on my watch. Of the three who still resisted, one was my Second squad leader. I told the others to head back and I would stay and make sure these three returned in time. I made them leave at 10:30. As we walked back, they were about 10 steps ahead of me. About halfway back to the barracks, they turned around and charged me. My first thought was take one out as quick as possible and deal with the other two. The first one to reach me got popped right between the eyes with a right jab and fell to the ground. The other two took me down and threw a few punches.

Just then I heard two people yelling, "What's going on?" It was the other two squad leaders coming back to help me at the club. They had seen that I had my hands full with these three clowns. The delinquents had scattered like rats by then, but once back at the barracks one of them came up and pushed me. That's all I needed. I grabbed him and threw him on the floor and started pounding his face. The other guys had to pull me off.

I guess I felt like I was finally at a place in my life where I was respected. I was judged only by my accomplishments and not the choices my parents made… and I liked that respect. It made me want to work hard. When these three disrespected me, I snapped. I had to prove that I was in charge. I had to stand up for the authority that was given to me. The next day, two of the guys tried to press charges against me. Our Lieutenant heard the story and told them that they were lucky that I am not pressing charges against *them!*

Basic training was ending in a few days. We would all go on to our next assignment and move on with our military careers. I was given leave for a week, so I got a plane ticket home. It was really nice to see everyone again. I spent the afternoons with Neil and the Bees, and the evenings with my friends.

There were plenty of parties to go to. I hadn't been able to get in touch with Joan yet, but one day I had to run to Glen's Market for Neil. As I walked through the door, I was thinking, "I hope Joan is working." I didn't see her at first, so I walked around the store. Pretty soon I heard a familiar voice, "Hey, stranger!" Sure enough, it was Joan, looking just as beautiful as I remember.

"I heard you were back in town and I was hoping that you would call or something," she said.

We talked for a bit, but she had to get back to work. I asked if she could get together after work, but she said she was leaving for a spring break trip to Mexico the next day. My heart sank. I was going away for a long time; I didn't know when—or even if—I'd ever see her again.

At Fort Gordon, I threw myself into my service, focusing on being a better soldier, and a better man. I knew that I had to start planning for my life after the Army and I really wanted to go to college. I signed up for the VEAP (Veteran's Education Assistance Program) and started contributing money to it each month.

AIT (Advanced Individual Training) went by really fast. I was a combat telecommunications specialist. Now that we were finished with basic training, we'd work from 6 a.m. to 5 p.m., but the weekends were ours.

In June I started jump school, a four-week course. The first week was conditioning, the second was ground training, the third week was jump training, and during the fourth week we jumped.

Summer time was hot in southern Georgia. For a boy from northern Michigan, 90 degrees was not so comfortable. We had to wear full Army uniforms and run and do PT most of the first week. Sometimes we'd walk through outside showers that were about 10 feet long to cool us down. There were horse troughs full of iced water to help revive the occasional soldier who passed out.

I remember my first jump like it was yesterday. We jumped from 2,500 feet out of a C-141. The jumpmaster yelled, "10 minutes!" It was cool inside the aircraft, but once the door opened, I could feel the hot air hit me.

"Stand up!" he yelled. "Hook up!" he further instructed.

The whole time I was thinking, *"What the heck am I doing?"*

I could feel the adrenaline rushing through my body. The next thing you know, we were rushed to the door.

"Go, Go, Go, Go!!! AIRBORNE ROOOOAAAAR!!!"

My heart was racing. Out the door I went! I looked up to check my chute and saw that the risers were twisted. I had to bicycle out, but within seconds I was floating to the ground.

It was the most exhilarating thing I had ever done in my life!

I looked for the smoke canisters on the ground. They are put there to show us the wind direction and also give us an idea of the wind speed by observing how fast the smoke is moving. I remember floating and thinking, "This is great!"

Then I had to prepare to land, which you do about 100 feet from the ground. You turn into the wind, bend your knees, and look at the horizon. Once you hit, you do a parachute-landing fall.

It all happened so fast—and I could not wait until the next one! I made a few more jumps that week, the last one at night. After that, with the jump training complete, it was off to Fort Bragg, my permanent station for the next two-and-a-half years.

I was assigned to A Co. 82nd Signal Battalion Commcenter Platoon. We had our first jump a week later. SPC-4 Venzke was my squad leader, and he was a real character. Your first jump is called a "cherry blast;" you're known as a "cherry" until your first jump. Some soldiers can go weeks or months before their first jump, and have to put up with being called a "cherry" the whole time. Fortunately, I got mine over the second week.

Venzke made it his mission to haze me during the entire process. He was behind me in our stick (the line you're in as you board and exit the plane), which meant that he'd be checking my equipment. He kept telling me, "I'm gonna cut your line, cherry! You're gonna crash and burn!"

Just before we were getting ready to load the plane, Venzke got called out of our stick by our platoon Sergeant. I asked the trooper behind me to save a spot and he agreed. When Venzke boarded the plane, I yelled, "Hey, Specialist! I saved your seat!"

He stopped and laughed and then came and sat down. He told me that I had balls, but I wasn't so smart because he was still going to cut my line. "You better know how to use your reserve," he said.

With that, we were off. The jump was from only 1,000 feet. Needless to say, Venzke did not cut my line, and from that point on, we were the best of friends. He would leave the Army a year before me, but we remain close to this day.

In August, I got a 17-day leave. I couldn't wait to get home! It was the prime of summer in East Jordan, and I had the money and time to enjoy it. Jackie and Duane picked me up at the airport, and we went directly to one of our friend's house for a party.

The days were spent on Lake Charlevoix on my friend Doug's boat; the nights were spent partying. There was always one going on, whether it was at Apple Tree Hill, The Dam, The Fishing Site, Webster's Bridge, or over someone's house.

Jump School, Ft. Benning, GA, June 1980

On the night before I had to get back to Fort Bragg, my friends and I went to a party at Apple Tree Hill. When we arrived, there were already about 100 kids there, and the bash was in full swing. I started pouring myself a beer out of the keg and someone came up behind me, covered my eyes and asked, "Guess Who?" in a disguised voice.

"Hi Joan" I said.

"How did you know it was me?"

I laughed and said as I turned around, "Because you're the only one who does that to me. If you really want to surprise me, next time walk up and give me a big kiss. That should leave me speechless for a while. Besides, you still owe me at least 500 kisses for my birthday."

She giggled and said that she'd keep that in mind. We walked over to my friend's truck and sat on the tailgate and talked for a while. I could have spent the entire evening talking to Joan. We talked about our old study hall class and how much fun we had. She asked how I was doing and seemed genuinely interested in what I had to say. She said she missed talking to me on the phone and that softball was not the same without me being there. She did point out that they were finally in first place though, laughing as she did.

Joan was so easy to talk to. She was so caring and genuine. She talked about getting through her senior year and then heading off to college. She was really looking forward to the next chapter in her life. She wasn't sure what school she'd attend yet, but had a few places in mind.

I could see now that my chance of ever having a relationship with Joan was a long shot at best. She would go off to college and meet some good-looking, rich kid studying pre-med or something, get married and live happily ever after. I knew it was time to just accept that we would never be anything more than friends.

CHAPTER 10

Fort Bragg

Once back at Fort Bragg, it occurred to me that baseball season was just six months away. I started working out every day—running at least 4 miles, doing push-ups and pull-ups, and lifting weights. This was in addition to the PT we were required to do every morning. Before long, I was in the best shape of my life. I quit smoking cigarettes and cut way back on drinking.

Things were going very well. I had never in my life felt more confident about my future and about my abilities as a man. I began taking classes at night to get a jump on the college courses that I'd take once I got out of the Army.

I wasn't able to get leave for Christmas; I was still the new guy and had to wait my turn. I was able to go home in early January. I only took 7 days, as I knew it would be very cold up north, and a week would most likely be enough.

Duane and Jackie picked me up at the airport in Pellston. They dropped me off at Neil's, then came back later to pick me up for a party at a friend's house. On the way there, Duane asked if there was any way I could come back the week of March 7th. "I think so—why?" I asked. "We want you to be in our wedding." Duane said.

"What? Heck, yeah!!" I said. "Congratulations!!"

My two best friends seemed very happy, and I was happy, too.

On Saturday, I went to another party, this time with my friend Tim. We played euchre—a popular card game in the Midwest. After a few hands, I went to get a refill on my beer. As I walked through the living room, there was Joan. Her face lit up as soon as she saw me, as did mine.

We quickly moved through the crowd to meet in the middle of the room. We talked for a few minutes. Then I informed her that the total number of kisses she owed me was up to at least 700. "You really should start chipping away at that," I said.

She smiled, then put her arms around my neck and pulled me

to her. We kissed. A really, really *great* kiss. We separated and looked at each other.

"How was that?" she asked.

I was stunned. "I think I need to go take a cold shower now," I said.

"Well, that should take at least a hundred away from what I owe you," she laughed.

"Nope, just one," I said.

She laughed again. We talked for a while and I told her that I'd be coming back in March for Duane and Jackie's wedding. After a while, Joan got back to her friends, and I got back to my card game. It was hard to concentrate, though; I couldn't stop thinking about Joan… and that kiss.

I didn't see her the rest of the week; she had to work, and I didn't want to push it. Before I knew it, it was time to get back to Fort Bragg.

A couple of weeks later, SPC4 Ortiz called me into his office. My first thought was, "What did I do now?" He sat me down and asked how I was doing. "Great… I think?" He laughed and proceeded to tell me about "Recondo" school, a two-and-a-half week training program at Fort Bragg. (The name comes from "reconnaissance" and "doughboy," an informal term for an American soldier.) Run by the Delta Force, it was one of the toughest in the Army.

It's a highly prestigious honor to graduate from Recondo school. Our battalion had sent several soldiers, but no one had made it past the first week. Our Lieutenant Colonel was not happy about this, and he was eager to find a soldier who could finish the program—soon. SPC4 Ortiz said that he told Lt. Col. Grey that he has just the person in mind.

"So they were asking *me* to go to this Recondo school?" I thought. "And not only go—but pass?"

SPC4 Ortiz told me that if I were successful, he'd personally nominate me for SPC4 rank. It was an amazing opportunity—but it would kill my chances of playing baseball, and that was the whole reason I joined the Army. If I did the school, I wouldn't be back in time for team tryouts.

I felt honored that SPC4 Ortiz believed in me, and I was eager to take on the challenge. I made a commitment to do the Recondo program, thinking I'd find a way to do baseball, too. But if it came down to one or the other, I'd keep my word to SPC4 Ortiz and give up my baseball dream.

He thanked me and said, "Don't let me down, Burch. You are representing the whole 82nd Signal Battalion."

What have I gotten myself in to *this* time?

I continued with my workouts, holding out hope that there'd be a way to do both baseball and Recondo school. I had a month to come up with a way to make it work. I put in a leave request for Jackie and Duane's wedding. I was really looking forward to going home, and to being a groomsman. They were the first of my friends to get married, and the first wedding I was ever in.

The flight from North Carolina had a four-hour layover in Chicago at O'Hare International Airport. A year earlier, in 1980, President Reagan had restored the 82nd Airborne Division's right to wear the maroon beret. (The Special Forces wore green and the Rangers wore black.) It was an honor to wear the uniform of the 82nd Airborne; our dress greens were exceptionally impressive.

When I arrived at O'Hare, I walked through the concourse in my uniform, feeling a great sense of pride. People were looking and pointing at me. I decided to have lunch and a beer in a pub, as I had several hours before my connecting flight. As I walked in, I noticed five sailors sitting at a table in the corner. They had probably just graduated from basic training at Great Lakes Naval Base, north of Chicago. I knew that because Jeff had joined the Navy, and went through boot camp there.

I finished my lunch, had a shot of Schnapps and took a drink of beer. The bartender took away my empty plate and shot glass, and set up five more shots of Schnapps and five more beers in front of me. The table of sailors had decided to buy me a drink... or five.

As I raised a shot glass to them, they loudly cheered. I drank it down, and then the next... and the next... and the next, until they were all gone. The sailors' cheers got louder with every shot. After downing the Schnapps, I walked over to their table and thanked them, as they left to go catch their flight. Then I went to work on the beer.

Needless to say, I slept the entire flight from Chicago to Traverse City—all 30 minutes of it. Duane's sister was waiting for me in Traverse City, and would drive me to East Jordan. She took one look at me and asked if I had been drinking. "Funny you should ask," I answered, and relayed the story about the sailors. I don't know if it was the story itself, or my inability to tell it, but she didn't seem to find any humor in it—at all.

Saturday, March 7, was warm and sunny day—unseasonably so for that time of year in northern Michigan. Jackie and Duane's wedding was beautiful, and I couldn't have been happier for two of my best friends to begin their lives together.

The reception was held at the local American Legion hall. After dinner, the party really got started. After dancing for a while, I went outside to cool off and have a smoke (an indulgence I allowed myself just for that weekend). Once back inside, I headed for the bar to get a beer. As I walked down the stairs, I saw Joan. She turned toward me and smiled.

As we walked toward each other and stopped, she reached out and hugged me and then kissed me on the cheek. "That brings you down to 748," I said, pulling the random number out of the air. She just laughed and said, "So, are you going to ask me to dance, or what?"

I grabbed her hand and walked through the crowd, up the steps and onto the dance floor. The song stopped just as we arrived. I remember praying that the next song would be a slow song so I could take her in my arms. God must have been listening, because "Special Lady" by Ray, Goodman & Brown came on.

"Somehow I knew it would be you… to change my gray skies to blue. And it was strange when you called my name… ever since that day I haven't been the same."

As the song played, we spent the dance looking at each other and talking. She told me she had decided to go to Aquinas College in Grand Rapids, Mich. "You should come visit me there sometime," she said. I told her about baseball, and the possibility of missing tryouts due to the training course.

It felt wonderful to be in Joan's arms. There was none of that awkwardness you sometimes feel when you're slow-dancing with someone. Everything was always so easy with Joan. She could melt my heart with just a glance.

We danced a few more times that evening, and then she had to leave. I was so grateful for the chance to spend some time with Joan, but I believed in my heart that it would be the last. I wouldn't be back home again before she went off to college, where her life would no doubt take a new direction. It was the end of hope for me, but I was OK with that. I just wanted her to be happy. She deserved to have a better life than what I'd be able to provide.

The following Monday, I arrived back at Fort Bragg. About a month later, I was on bus heading to the Recondo training area.

We started the first week with about 120 soldiers, including 30 Marines who had come from Camp Lejeune.

When we arrived, the party had already started. The officers were yelling and cursing and telling us to get moving. They directed us to where we'd be camping for the next 17 days. No barracks—we would sleep outside for the duration, from April 7 through April 24th.

As we were put in formation, the officers went over the things we would be learning: map reading, land navigation, patrolling techniques, military demolitions, communications, first aid, combat intelligence, and, last but not least, SERAE training (survival, evasion, resistance, and escape). We had to sign a waiver for prisoner of war training, as this would be a hands-on experience—meaning that you would be beaten and interrogated.

The first task was to fill sandbags to put in the backpacks we'd wear on our runs. The sandbags were required to weigh at least 60 pounds. They must never fall below 60 pounds, so we all filled ours to weigh 65 pounds, to compensate for any leakage.

The next morning, we were up at 6 a.m. for PT. Stretching, push-ups, sit-ups, jumping jacks, and then a 5-mile run with our 60-pound sand bags, plus our weapons in port arms position all the way.

We lost a quarter of the group in the first three days.

For the first two weeks, we followed the same routine: After PT, we'd get chow, then have classroom training until lunch. We'd practice what we learned after lunch, and then have dinner, followed by more classroom training.

During the first week, we were driven out into the woods, given a map and compass and a set of grid coordinates. We were split up in to teams of three men. The object was to get from Point A to Point B. Each team was dropped off at a different location, but we all had the same finish line. Each course was 10 kilometers long, in a very thick forest, and we had to be back in two-and-a-half hours. My team finished in two hours.

After that task, we had our dinner of combat rations and started our night patrol. We finished at midnight, and had to be back up at 6 a.m. for PT. It was a long day, to say the least.

The next day, we learned to rappel off a 50-foot tower. That was actually a lot of fun! The following day, we learned about military demolitions, which taught us about explosives. While in class, the Sergeant took some C-4s and shaped them into a sculpture of sorts, then tossed it out into the classroom. We all scattered like flies as it fell to the floor. We waited for it to explode, but nothing happened. The Sergeant started laughing and informed us that a C-4 needs something to make it explode, like a blasting cap. After that initial scare, it was a lot of fun when we went outside and were able to blow up a bunch of things.

One day, after PT, the officers told us it was game day. I was sure it wasn't going to be as fun as it sounded. We were led over to a big hole in the ground, about 60 feet in diameter. It was about 3 feet deep, and lined with sand bags. The name of the game was "Bear Pit."

They had all of us soldiers—about 50 of us remained—get into the pit, then they explained the rules. The object of the game was to be the last one in the pit. To eliminate opponents, you had to get their feet above the level of the pit. Which basically meant that you had to flip them upside down and get them out of the hole. Some of us worked as a team to eliminate the Marines, which worked well. But in the end, it was every man for himself. I did well, until I took a knee right to the schnoz. Instantly, there was blood flowing from my nose and tears coming from my eyes. It was the first time I had ever broken my nose, and I had two shiners for the remainder of the program.

A few days later, while patrolling, our entire class was ambushed. We were separated and blindfolded. Our hands were duct-taped together; we were stripped of our boots, and the laces were used to tie us together.

We were marched for an hour or so, in different directions, so as to confuse us. I desperately tried to keep my bearings, but it was useless.

We arrived at the "POW" camp around noon. We were stripped of our shirts and pants, and made to kneel under the hot sun with our arms straight at our sides. If anyone tried to look around or peek out of their blindfold, they'd be smacked or get a swift kick. I could hear other soldiers being hit and screaming. Music from the Far East was blaring the entire time.

I had been in this position for what seemed to be about an hour, when I was grabbed and dragged into a room. Still blindfolded, I was repeatedly asked questions about my mission and who my leaders were and their names and ranks. I repeated my name and rank and Social Security Number time after time, question after question... but revealed nothing more.

My "captors" started pouring water on me and hitting me—really hard! This went on for almost an hour, and then they dragged me back out into the hot sun, where I was made to kneel again.

I would get one more round of interrogation, but that was it for me. The torture went on for two straight days. On the evening of the second night, all of us "prisoners" escaped.

At this point, we only had one more test... the final test. It consisted of 50 push-ups with the 60-pound sand bags on our backs, 15 pull-ups, 50 sit-ups, while holding your weapon in your hands above your head; and a 5-mile run with the sand bag.

The night before the final test, I got sick. To this day, I'm convinced that I had the flu. I was hot and cold all night long, and threw up a few times. I guess it could have been heat exhaustion, but I really think it was the flu. The next morning, I knew that I had to finish this test, sick or not. There was no way that I was going to give up after making it this far. I was still sweating and freezing, but made it through the push-ups, pull-ups, and barely through the sit-ups. I had about 20 minutes to rest while everyone else finished. Then came the run.

I was in the middle of the pack for most of the way. But about a mile from the finish, I started to feel really bad. I went to the side of the trail and began violently throwing up. I fell to my knees, and it just kept coming. By the time I was finished, the rest of the pack was about 50 yards ahead.

I told myself, *"I will not quit!"* I shakily got up and ran as fast as I could, vomited one last time while running, and caught up with the group. About a quarter-mile from the end, I resumed my position in the middle of the pack, which I held until the end.

I made it!! I walked around in circles for a while and came to my senses. *It was over—and I made it!*

We spent the rest of the day cleaning up our sleep area and equipment. At a graduation ceremony the next day, we were presented with a certificate of completion and a medal, the kind with a pin-

back. In keeping with tradition, the Sergeant put the medal in my hand and stabbed me with the pin, as he shook my other hand.

(In jump school, we got "blood wings." When the officer pinned your wings on your chest, he pushed it into your chest through your shirt. Hence "blood wings." This was the same concept.)

I opened my hand and looked down at my bloodied medal with pride. I still have a small scar on the palm of my right hand, which to this

Shortly after RECONDO school,
Ft. Bragg, N.C. - 1981

day reminds me to never give up when pursuing a goal.

Thirty-two of us graduated from the Recondo program—out of the more than 120 soldiers who began it. It was the proudest moment of my life. I was a man now, and I could do anything I put my mind to.

Although I was disappointed about not being able to try out for the baseball team, Recondo school was worth it, and I had no regrets. Lt. Col. Grey called me into his office and personally expressed his gratitude. I was extremely proud of my accomplishment.

A couple of months later, my good friend and fellow soldier SPC4 Sean Luketina from the 82nd Signal Battalion, would go on to complete the Recondo program as well. (Sean would later die—just one day shy of his 24th birthday—as a result of injuries suffered in a friendly fire incident during Operation Urgent Fury in Grenada.)

No one in the outside world could possibly understand what a difficult challenge this was. None of my civilian friends seemed all that impressed. But I knew what I had accomplished, and that's all that mattered.

CHAPTER 11

The Letter

Before I joined the Army, I was directionless. I had no goals or plan... no idea who I was or what I wanted to become. For most of my life, I was too busy just trying to survive! I spent my first 15 years trying to overcome one tragedy after another, and a series of people who destroyed my confidence.

After I went to live with Neil, I was more on cruise control, still just surviving. Although my confidence improved, there was something missing. I couldn't figure out what it was until I joined the Army. That experience taught me that I could do and have whatever I set my mind to... and let me tell you, I had a pocket full of dreams.

I had courage; I wouldn't have survived my childhood without it. What I didn't have was respect. Respect cannot be granted or bestowed upon you. You have to earn it through your character, your accomplishments, and your actions as a person. It starts with respecting yourself; if you don't respect yourself, how can you expect other people to respect you?

Courage and respect are huge in life. They're the very core of who a person becomes, and to have them is a great accomplishment. But *honor*—honor is the end result of courage and respect. It's what all great people strive for. Honor is what I found in the Army. I often hear how underpaid soldiers are, which is true, if you're talking about money. But for me, the Army gave something that money cannot buy—respect and honor.

When I got back to the Signal Battalion after Recondo training, I went straight to my room to take a shower and get cleaned up. I planned on enjoying the day off before getting back to regular Army life. My roommate, Mikey, was sitting in the room watching TV when I arrived. I still had the remnants of two black eyes and a cracked nose. He just looked at me as I dropped my stuff by my bunk. As I took off my shirt to head to the shower, Mikey could see the bruises on my back, chest, and stomach where I had been beaten.

"What the heck??" Mikey said. "What happened to you—you get in a car accident? Fall off a tall building, or what?"

I explained, and he was dumbfounded by it all.

I received a few letters from Joan in the following months. The tone of her writing seemed to have changed. I really felt that when we had that slow dance at Jackie and Duane's wedding reception, something happened... something sparked. But it appeared to be just wishful thinking on my part.

SPC4 Ortiz kept his promise, and I was promoted to SPC4 after just 16 months, unusually quick for the 82nd Airborne. During those 16 months, I had done more to become a man... I had learned more about myself, and what I wanted to become, than in all of the previous 20 years of my life combined. The Army taught me that the little guy, a nobody, *does* have a chance—a chance to change his life and control his destiny.

I went home on leave at Christmas, flying to Toledo first and hooking up with my old buddy Venzke. He and I were going to drive up to East Jordan together, then head to Rockford, Mich., where Jackie and Duane had moved. Venzke's mom made a big pot of chili for us for dinner; the next morning, we jumped in the car and headed north.

After we got into town, we headed straight for a high school basketball game, and then went to Neil's house. Barb asked if we were hungry. "We're starving," I said.

"Good" she said, "Because I made chili".

The next day we headed to Rockford, about a four-hour drive, to see Duane and Jackie. When we arrived, Jackie was in the kitchen making dinner for us all. Guess what she made? Chili! Venzke and I just looked at each other and laughed.

We all took a trip to Grand Rapids, Mich., to pick up our old friend Pat from college. Pat told me that Joan's school was only a few miles down the road. "You should call her," she said.

I mustered up the courage and called. We chatted for a minute, and then I invited her to come back to Jackie and Duane's with us. There was silence on the other end of the phone for what seemed like an eternity, then I could hear the discomfort in her voice.

"David, I'm sorry. I have a date tonight," she said. "I wish I would have known you were coming, I would have loved to see you.

But I've already made plans."

"No, that's OK. I know it was last minute. I should have written to you. Maybe I'll see you in East Jordan."

Unfortunately, I didn't get to see her at all that leave. I heard she met someone in college… just as I had feared. I knew it was over now, and it broke my heart. For some reason, deep inside I believed that the fairy tale would come true… that somehow we would get married and live happily ever after. I had to accept that it wasn't going to happen; I had to move on.

That Christmas, there was a different atmosphere at Neil's house. It didn't feel like my home anymore; I felt more like a visitor. Neil had married Barb, and they had formed a new family. Barb had children, and Neil's family life now revolved around her family and the Bees.

As a blended family, we drew names and were to spend $15 dollars on a gift for the person whose name we had drawn. We would all get together on Christmas Eve and exchange gifts. I went ahead and bought a presents for Neil and Barb, the Bees and others. There were a lot of presents under the tree!

When it was time to open gifts, I was given one to unwrap. I carefully removed the paper and opened the box. Inside was a pair of suspenders in the color of the rainbow—the kind Robin Williams wore on *Mork and Mindy*. The kind you could probably pick up at K-Mart for $1.99. I faked a smile and thanked the person who gave them to me. It would be the only Christmas gift I received that year.

It may sound a little melodramatic, but it really told me where I stood in life. I was on my own now, and not really a part of any family. It hurt me deeply and I felt so alone.

Have you ever seen the movie *Officer and a Gentleman?* There's a scene where Lou Gossett Jr.'s character tells Richard Gere's Zack Mayo that he's kicked out of the military. Mayo breaks down and says, *"I got nowhere to go… (sobbing)… I got nowhere to go!"*

What he was saying was that he had no home other than the military. That's exactly how I felt. Even today, it chokes me up to see that scene.

Back at Fort Bragg, I started hanging out with a guy named James Kogy Peacock. He was an American citizen, but was originally from Japan. His father had been in the Navy. James was a pitcher and stood about 6 ft.-1 in tall. I told him that I was going to try out for the baseball team in February, and that he should, too. We started working out together, mostly playing catch. I also worked out on my own, lifting weights and running. James had a great arm. He threw a 90 mile-per-hour fastball. His forkball was in the mid 70s, and fell off the table just before the plate.

After the first day of tryouts, I was really worried. There were more than 100 guys trying for only eight to 10 spots. James was

Conference at the mound with James – Spring 1982

a shoe-in. I, on the other hand, was not so confident. They only needed one catcher, as their starter from last year, Torez, was coming back.

Coach Santana told me that I was second out of six, but unfortunately, they were only keeping one catcher. Thinking fast, I told him that I could play other positions just as well. He had me go to second, then third, then the outfield. After tryouts, he told me that he really liked what he saw. He said that he'd like to have one guy on the team that he felt comfortable putting at in any position—and that he would like that player to be me. I made the team!

Shortly before baseball season was to start, I had to go on a field mission to the Mojave Desert and would be gone for 30 days. I was really disappointed to have to miss the start of the season, but Coach said not to worry: "Army comes first. Baseball, second."

The mission was called "Gallant Eagle '82." It was the first time that the Rapid Deployment Force would do a joint mission all at once. There were 2,200 jumpers and 90 aircraft over the Mojave Desert in one massive jump and drop. We also dropped 200 tons of equipment.

I was in the advanced mission, so we went in to set up base and communication two days before the invasion. It was a mock war.

I was in charge of the communications center, along with Sgt. Jenkins. We could see all the aircraft, and messages were coming in fast and furious. Our battalion was in charge of all communication for the headquarters of the 82nd Airborne, which included all of the top commanders. Needless to say, there was tension in our tent.

Ten minutes before the invasion, the Teletypes were running like I had never seen before. Then all of a sudden, everything went quiet.

There were three different drop zones for all 2,200 jumpers. One was called the "Rock Drop Zone." It was set up on a high part of the desert, with mountains on either side. The winds were being measured at 8-10 knots, but when the jump happened, they had picked up to 20-30 knots. That's way too high.

The jump was well under way. Another half-an-hour passed, and it was so quiet, you could hear a pin drop. Suddenly, we could hear the radio guys begin to talk loudly outside of our tent. Our Teletypes lit up like a Christmas tree. I heard a radio guy say "Three dead, 25 injured on the Rock!" I said, "What?? This isn't real, right? This is part of the drill."

"Four dead, 75 injured," came over the Teletype. I kept thinking, "This *has* to be made up." Only it wasn't. The winds were too high that day to be jumping. One soldier was dragged to his death, one was scalped, and another landed in the Heavy Drop Zone, where we drop tanks and trucks and other heavy equipment. There were numerous broken bones. In the end, six died and more than 150 were injured.

On the way back to Fort Bragg, we had to make a quick stop at Marsh Air Force Base in California. It was a 15- or 20-minute flight to get there. Sgt. Jenkins and I were the only two on board from the 82nd Signal Battalion. We took off fine, but the landing was something else. *Bam!* We hit hard and were skidding onto the runway.

As soon the plane stopped, we jumped up and looked out the window. There were several fire trucks and other equipment outside of our plane and people were running with fire hoses towards the landing gear. Jenkins and I ran toward the exit and got off to see them hosing down one tire. Turns out we had gotten a flat on takeoff. I was so happy to be out of that plane.

Once back in North Carolina, I went right to the baseball field in my Army Jeep. There was a game under way. James came walking up to talk to me, as he wasn't pitching that day. I had just come from 30+ days in the Mojave Desert, and my skin was dark and weathered. James said that I looked like a soldier of fortune or mercenary or something. He said that he hardly recognized me when I pulled up.

I talked to Coach Santana and he told me to come to Sunday's game ready to play. The second catcher had to quit and he needed me. He also told me that Torez had been promoted to E-6 and had to go to Non-commissioned Officer school for eight weeks, and that I'd be the starting catcher during that time.

This opened up the door for me. While we were playing against UNC-Wilmington, there was a scout from Florida watching. I had a really good game, and afterward, he talked to me and asked if I'd be interested in coming to Florida and playing for his semi-professional summer team.

I told him that I wouldn't be getting out of the Army until January of 1983. He gave me his card and told me to call him in February. He said the team starts in April, and he'd like me there. He told me that he worked with two colleges in Florida, and thought that he could get me into one of them. Even though it was a whole year away, I was excited. My baseball dreams were coming true.

In June, my brother Jeff informed me that he was getting married. He was still in the Navy and was stationed in Meridian, Miss. The wedding was planned for July. I put in for a seven-day leave, and was looking forward to seeing my brother on his special day. I was granted the leave, but because I had spent a lot of money on my car the month before and it still wasn't running, I was really low on funds. I decided to hitchhike the 650+ miles to Mississippi. I was picked up by a trucker heading to Texas, who was able to take me all the way to Meridian. What luck!

Jeff's bride was a cute girl named Vickie. She came from an upper-class family—definitely out of our league. She had a friend named Pam, who I was matched up with at the wedding. We got along well, and people kept joking about what a great couple we'd make. We spent a lot of time together over the long weekend. The night of the reception, after many rounds of drinks, someone said that Pam and I should be the next to get married. I jokingly said, "I agree! Let's get hitched!" To my disbelief, she said, "OK!"

"Wait... I didn't mean that," I thought to myself.

The next day, I told Pam that if she wanted to be engaged, we could be. But we needed to slow things down, as we had only known each other for four days. She agreed.

On the train ride back to Fort Bragg, I had a lot of time to think. "This is ridiculous," I told myself. "I can't marry Pam." But I couldn't stop thinking about how good Jeff's life was, and how well he was doing. Vickie's family had money. Pam's family had money. For the few days she and I were together, I had it made. Whenever we went out, I drove her dad's Lincoln Town Car. Wherever we ate or whatever we did, it was put on her dad's tab. I was living a life I had never lived before, where money was no object. Pam's dad told me that he had connections at a local junior college that had a pretty good baseball team; he also had connections at Auburn.

I decided to try to make this relationship work. Why not? I couldn't have Joan, the only girl I ever loved. I didn't love Pam, but maybe I could learn to.

Back at Fort Bragg, it was back to the routine. I tried to talk to Pam as often as I could, but still wasn't really feeling the spark. James was getting ready to get out of the service, and I was able to buy his 1965 Buick Wildcat. I loved that car!

Five days after I got back from Jeff's wedding, I received a letter from Joan. It began, "My Dearest David B."

Her words startled me. We hadn't talked since December of 1981, when I was in Grand Rapids but she couldn't see me, because she had a date. And we hadn't seen each other in more than a year.

She wrote that it had seemed like ages since we had been in touch, and that she found herself thinking about me a lot, and that she really missed me. She made a reference to our old study hall class and how those were the "good ol' days." At the end of the letter, she called me "sweetheart." Then there was the P.S., which read, "You haven't forgot about our wedding already, have you??"

This was a lot to take in. Was she serious? Just when I thought there was no way I would ever have a chance with Joan, I get this letter.

I waited a few days to write back. I needed time to process things and figure out how I was going to respond. I decided to lay it on the line.

I wrote to Joan and told her how much I loved her letter. I told her that I wasn't in a relationship with anyone at this time, and asked her if she wanted to be my girlfriend. I sent the letter off, held my breath and waited for a reply.

It came in just a few days. I couldn't believe it. She wrote that she was interested in being more than just friends with me. The rest of the summer of 1982, we talked on the phone a few times a month and wrote to each other just as frequently. Each letter and phone conversation got more and more flirtatious. It seemed as though things were moving along perfectly.

Over Labor Day weekend, my buddy Mikey and I went to Meridian, Miss. to visit Jeff. On the drive there, I thought about how I was going to break it off with Pam. About an hour after we arrived, I just came out and told her that it wasn't going to work. I had wanted to wait to tell her in person. Our relationship, which had never been built on anything of substance, ended just as quickly as it began.

I spent the rest of the weekend fishing with Jeff and Mikey. It was a great sense of relief to no longer worry about marrying someone I didn't love. More important, it was looking as if I might finally have a chance with the girl of my dreams. I had fallen in love with Joan the very first time I met her, all those years ago.

My phone bills, from all of those talks with Joan, were astronomical, but I didn't care. Many times when I called, her roommate, Patti would answer. It was fun getting to know her and I looked forward to meeting her. Joan and I adopted the song "Truly" by Lionel Ritchie as our song. Never in my life had I been so happy.

One night in mid-December, we were on the phone. I was going in for ear surgery the next day to correct a problem that had been bothering me for a year or so. During the conversation, I asked Joan to marry me. I told her I could re-enlist in the Army, and she could move to North Carolina. There was a long period of silence, and then she shot me down.

"I think we're moving too fast, Dave. Let's just see how things go when you come home."

Her feelings still hadn't caught up to mine.

I had the ear surgery and was in the hospital for three days. I tried to call Joan, but there was no answer. I tried again on Christmas Eve and on Christmas Day, with no luck. When I finally got ahold of her a few days later, she told me that she couldn't talk because she had company. It was one of her old boyfriends from middle school, but she said they were just friends. Joan then told me that she needed some time and that maybe it would be better if we didn't talk for a while.

I was devastated.

I didn't know what to make of Joan's sudden pullback. I gave her some space for a few days, and then on New Year's Eve, I had to call. We didn't talk long. She told me that she had gone to a basketball game earlier in the week with her old boyfriend, but again, just as friends. She said that when I asked her to marry her, it took her by surprise and the more she thought about it, the more confused she got. She told me that she just needed some time to think things through.

I wrote her a letter that day telling her how I felt and that I feared things had changed between us. I received a letter back from her, assuring me that nothing had changed... that she still loved and missed me, and that she couldn't wait until I got home. We resumed our relationship and started writing letters and talking on the phone, the same as before. I had saved about $1,800 to live on after I got out, until I could find a job.

On January 21, 1983, my three-year commitment to the U.S. Army was fulfilled. I was a free man.

CHAPTER 12

Grand Rapids

The plan was to drive to Venzke's in Toledo and spend the weekend. From there, I'd go to Detroit and stay with my grandmother until Thursday, and then to Grand Rapids to see Joan.

It was really good to see Venzke again, and we had a great visit. The time I was able to spend with my grandmother was very special, as she would live only a few more months before succumbing to cancer. I told her all about Joan and how I hoped that she was "the one." Grandma was very happy for me and told me how proud she was of me. She said that she knew how hard my childhood was, and that she was very glad that I was able to put that all behind me and move on in life. She was always there for me and I always wanted to make her proud. It felt very good to know that I had done that.

My Aunt Nonie and I went shopping, and she helped me pick out some cologne. "Joan will love this," she said.

It was driving me crazy that Joan was just three hours away, and I couldn't be with her until Thursday. She had to babysit in the evenings on Tuesday and Wednesday, which is why we decided that I should come on Thursday… but I just couldn't stand it any longer. I called her and told her that I needed to be with her, and could I come on Tuesday instead?

"I'll help you babysit," I said.

"Of course" she replied.

On Tuesday morning, my grandmother made me breakfast, and we talked for a bit. I told her that I was really sorry for leaving early, but she just laughed and said that she understood. She knew how eager I was to go see Joan. I put on my dress uniform, hoping that Joan would like the way I looked in it, and headed out.

At the beginning of December, I had purchased a Christmas present for Joan. At the time, I only had about $150 to spend, but knew that I wanted to get her a ring. I debated over getting an opal or a pearl. Would a pearl be too forward? Would an opal seem too subtle? How would she take getting a ring?

I went to a number of stores before finally deciding on an opal. I had told Joan that I wanted to give her the Christmas present in person, but now I was very nervous about doing so. She had, after all, turned down my marriage proposal. Driving to Grand Rapids, I couldn't help thinking maybe the ring was a bad idea. Maybe it would scare her away again.

The three-hour drive seemed to take forever. But I soon got into town and began looking for the college. Joan had given me directions, but I was so nervous I managed to drive right past it. I ended up finding a payphone and calling Joan. She got me turned around.

My heart was pounding so hard that I thought it would come right out of my chest. I pulled up to her dorm, grabbed the ring, put it in my pocket, and went in. I walked up to the front desk and asked to see Joan Swanson. The girl behind the desk made a phone call upstairs, and I waited. Words cannot express how nervous I was. A minute later, Joan walked through the door and came toward me with that beautiful smile. We hugged and then she kissed me. It wasn't a "welcome home, friend" kiss. It was a real kiss. *Wow!*

As we held each other, I savored every moment. My mind was spinning and I could feel the passion run through my body. Although I didn't want it to, the kiss ended and we separated. I wanted to just kiss and hold her forever. In her arms, I felt as though I had finally found a home.

We held hands and just looked at each other, and without really even thinking about it, I reached into my coat pocket and took out her Christmas present. As she lifted the lid and saw that it was a ring, I held my breath. She took one look at it, and then handed the box back to me.

My heart sunk.

Then she said, "What are you waiting for? Wouldn't the proper thing be for you to put this on my finger?"

Joan smiled and leaned in and kissed me. "I love it," she said.

She removed the ring she was wearing on her left ring finger, her class ring, and shifted it to her right hand. I then replaced it with her new opal.

We went upstairs to her dorm room so I could meet her roommate, Patti, then we headed to lunch. I asked Joan where she wanted to go. "I'll take you anywhere you want to go," I told her. "I want to go to Wendy's," she replied. That was our very first meal together. We spent several hours talking, and soon it was time for Joan to go to class. I hung out in the dorm room and waited for her, and then we left for her babysitting job. She watched two school-aged boys two days a week for a little extra income.

Joan helped them with their homework and made them dinner. I kept the boys busy while she cooked by playing Legos. Hanging out with kids came natural to me, as I was used to taking care of the Bees. In my mind, I was thinking what great parents Joan and I would make some day. We both loved kids.

Once the boys went to bed, Joan started working on her homework at the kitchen table, while I tried to watch TV. To tell you the truth, television was the furthest thing from my mind. I knew I had to talk to Joan and tell her how I felt, I just didn't know how.

Suddenly, she shut her book, got up, and came over to me. She sat down and put her head on my shoulder. She told me that she was so happy that we were finally together. We kissed several times, but I could not focus. I pulled away and told her that I had waited for this since I was 15 years old, and that it was the happiest day of my life. I then explained that I would go as fast or slow as she wanted in this relationship, but that I would marry her tomorrow if it were up to me.

"I know that you wanted to take this slow, so just tell me when you're ready," I said. "I will not bring it up again, so it will be up to you to tell me."

I had never been so happy. She told me that she had never loved someone the way she loved me. She said that she was afraid and excited all at the same time, because she had never had feelings like this. We started kissing again, and again my body was filled with desire. I never in my wildest dreams imagined how wonderful it would be to kiss her, hold her, and touch her. My mind was spinning, but I knew I had to stop before things went too far, and she would regret it.

I went to the kitchen and got myself a glass of cold water. After regaining my composure, I went back and sat with her on the couch. I told her I loved her too much to take advantage of her. "I know you're confused, and I don't want to do anything to mess this up."

She told me that she understood, and that she loved me.

We had known each other for so long, and over the past six months had developed a much closer bond through our letters and phone calls.

On the way back to the dorm, I told Joan that although it may have scared her in December when I asked her to marry me, I hope she understood that I was serious about what I asked. But for now, I didn't want her to feel any pressure. "I'm going to leave the door open," I said. "You tell me if and when you're ready."

She smiled and said that she had given it a lot of thought since I asked her in December, but would like to continue thinking about it. "Thank you for being patient with me, David," she said. "Let's just see how the next few months go."

I slept on the couch in Joan's dorm room for the next few nights. She introduced me to all of her friends, and we had a lot of fun. One sunny afternoon, I was alone in the room when Joan came back from class. She walked in and asked if I wanted to go to the cafeteria for lunch. "Sure," I said. I waited while she went into the bathroom to freshen up. "Ready, Freddie?" she said as she came out.

Just then, the song "Just You and I" by Eddie Rabbitt and Crystal Gayle came on the radio. Joan turned to me and said, "This is the song I was telling you about!" Our bodies came together at the center of the room and we danced. We were kissing passionately and fell onto the couch. We continued to kiss and touch and hold each other. After the song ended, Joan looked into my eyes and asked me if I believe in fate. She said that she thought we had to do the things we did in life to lead us to this point... this moment.

"Right here, right now... I believe it was meant to be. How else can you explain that in the summer some five years ago, you played a song for me at your house? Then later, you told me that someday you'd ask me to marry you. Then in study hall, you gave me a picture of a ring out of a magazine. You spent all of your money at the fair on a bracelet for me. I still have these things in my memory box. They're among my most prized possessions. And now, here we are, together."

Joan continued on, "My heart is pounding like a drum right now. I can't stop thinking of you. All morning, I sat in class and was just lost in my thoughts... thoughts of you and me and our future... thoughts of being Mrs. David Burch. I have never felt so close and comfortable and safe with someone, and I have never felt such a profound love. I have never wanted to do the things that I want to do with you."

"I'm ready, David," she said.

"Wait Joan, you're ready for what?" I asked. "Are you telling me that you will marry me?"

"Well, not until you ask me properly."

I got down on one knee, took her hand and looked deep in to her beautiful blue eyes. "Joan Michelle Swanson, I have never loved anyone as much as I love you. I fell in love with you the first day I met you at the beach in East Jordan. From that point on, I knew that you were the only one I wanted to spend the rest of my life with. Will you marry me?" As tears filled her eyes, she smiled and said, "Yes."

In a few days, I was leaving to go back to East Jordan. I couldn't continue living in the dorm room, and thought I could go back up north and perhaps get my old job back temporarily. Joan and I were still trying to figure out our future, whether it meant me rejoining the Army, going to Florida to play baseball, or staying in Grand Rapids and start our life together there. At any rate, Joan had to finish out the school year.

We were having a lot of fun going out in the evenings and hanging out with Joan's friends. There were a lot of great clubs and bars in Grand Rapids, and a lot of good food. A place within walking distance called Yesterdog quickly became a favorite. They have the *best* Coney Islands! Another favorite was a restaurant called Arnie's.

The days quickly passed. On Saturday, our last day together, we woke up early and planned our day. We decided to go shopping for wedding rings, and then go to a movie at The Woodland Mall. We didn't find just the right ring that day, but saw an afternoon flick: *Kiss Me Goodbye*, with Sally Field, James Caan, and Jeff Bridges. Joan and I got our tickets, pop, and popcorn and took our seats. A few minutes later, the lights went down and the previews started. The next thing I knew, I was being roused awake by an usher, the theater now empty and the lights all on.

I turned to Joan. "Did you like the movie?""

"I don't know," she giggled. "I slept through the whole thing!"

"Me too!!"

I guess the week of fun and the late nights had caught up with us. We went to dinner at Russ' on 28th Street and talked about what we'd do for the rest of the night. She talked about going back to campus and hanging out, or going out to a club. I told Joan that this was our last night together, and that I wanted to spend it with her—and only her. I went on to tell her that the past five days have been the most amazing five days of my life, and that I really didn't want to go back to East Jordan and leave her. I wanted to spend every minute of every day with her. Then I got up the courage to ask her what I had been thinking.

"Joan," I began. "What do you think about going back to your dorm room and packing a few things, then stopping at the store to get some beer and snacks, then getting a motel room?"

She tensed up and had a nervous smile on her face. "They're not going to let us get a room!"

I told her that my buddies and I have rented hotel rooms many times on trips to Florida. "There is no reason they won't give us a room, why wouldn't they? You stay in the car, and I'll get a room." I could see the nervousness on her face. But to my surprise, she said yes… she wanted to spend the night with me. She giggled and said, "I can't believe we are going to do this."

I drove up to The Cascade Inn, walked in and told the desk clerk that I needed a room. "For how many?" he asked.

"Um, what?"

"How many will be in the room?" he repeated.

"Uh, my wife and me," I said.

I was nervous and excited at the same time. My heart was pounding and it was hard to stand still. He asked for a major credit card, and when I said I didn't have one, he said that he could take $150 deposit, which I would get back upon checkout. He handed me the room key and I walked back to the car. Joan was looking at me curiously, wondering if I had pulled it off.

When I flashed her the room key, she laughed and said, "Oh Crap! You're kidding me! I can't believe we are doing this!!" She had never done or even thought about doing something like this. We were both still young and very naïve. This was all new to us. It seemed to take an eternity to go back to her dorm room and then the store. Finally, we arrived back at the motel room.

Joan looked so beautiful as she looked at me shyly. We started kissing passionately, and soon our clothes came off, one article at a time. It was extremely romantic, not rushed, but slow and exciting. I could feel her heart beating as I touched her, but everything came naturally. It was as though we belonged together. We spent the whole night in each other's arms, making love and talking about our future.

My plan was to go to East Jordan and work until I could rejoin the Army. Joan would finish out the school year, and I'd call the scout in Florida, thank him and tell him that I was giving up baseball for now. But for this night, we had each other... and it was amazing. I did not want the sun to come up. I wanted this night to last forever.

We fell asleep in the wee hours of the morning. After about two hours, I woke up and just sat there watching Joan sleep. I got dressed and left to buy her flowers and some breakfast. She was still sleeping when I returned, and I didn't want to wake her. I just wanted to look at her magnificent body. She looked like an angel. *My* angel.

The next day, it was time for me to leave. It was excruciating. I was so happy, but in my experience, when things are good, the world had a way of soon crashing around you. I was so worried because I didn't want to lose Joan.

On the long drive to East Jordan, I did a lot of thinking, about what had gotten me to this point in my life. How could a loser kid from a no-name family make it this far on his own? I thought about high school and the people who failed me and the people who would have loved to see me fail, but then I thought about the people who believed in me and helped me... Coach Jack, Mr. Brzozowy, Mr. Gee, Mr. Carpenter, and Mr. Burrows.

I thought about my exceptional military career and the people who helped turn a misunderstood boy into a man. I thought about jump school, Recondo school, baseball, and other things I had accomplished during those three years. Then I thought of Joan.

I had wanted to impress her and win her love from day one. Now that I had, I couldn't disappoint her. I needed to be better than I had been. I needed to work harder to provide the kind of life she deserved. The kind of life *I* deserved. The kind of life our future children deserved.

My car was going 55 m.p.h., but my mind was going 155! I could hardly keep up with my thoughts. I really wanted to go to college, but I didn't know what kind of major I'd pursue. I prayed for some guidance.

Joan asked me if I believed in fate. I didn't know how I felt about fate. I knew that up until that point, many things in my life had not worked out the way I would have liked. Whenever I got comfortable with something, it went away. But now Joan has agreed to be my wife. I had to believe it was meant to be.

Once back in East Jordan, I visited with Neil and the Bees, and stopped in to see some friends. They were all happy when I told them that Joan and I were getting married. Over the next several days, I worked on getting a job. Although the economy had started to recover, I wasn't having any luck. I missed Joan terribly. It seems once I kissed her and held her in my arms, my whole world changed. I woke up thinking about her, went through the day thinking of her, and went to bed thinking of her. We made plans for her to come to East Jordan to celebrate my 22nd birthday in February.

That weekend, we spent every minute together. We hung out with Joan's family. Her sister Teri and her husband had us over for dinner and a game of cards. They were great. Joan's younger brother, Dan, and I played catch—even though there was still snow on the ground. I also met Joan's older sister Pat.

I got along well with Joan's mom. All those years of calling her house when we were in high school gave me plenty of opportunity to score points with her. I loved to flirt with her and make her blush.

Joan's father, on the other hand, I did not know at all. By the way he looked at me, I could tell that he was going to be a tough nut to crack.

Her parents had no idea how much Joan and I loved each other, or how far our relationship had gone. On Sunday, I asked if I could have a minute alone with them. The three of us sat down in the living room. I was shaking on the inside, but tried to appear confident. "I am in love with your daughter, and have asked her to marry me," I said. "She has agreed to be my wife, but I would like to ask for your permission."

Joan's dad challenged, "What are you going to do if we say no?"

"Sonny, stop," Joan's mom said.

I replied, "I love her. I will take care of her, and hope we have your approval."

Joan's father looked at me for a minute, and then stood up and shook my hand.

That afternoon, Joan had to head back to Grand Rapids. The weekend had gone by way too fast. It felt as though my heart was being ripped out... again.

Within two days, I packed my car and followed her there. I was homeless and jobless, but I couldn't stay away from her any longer.

I had about $600 left from the money I had saved, but had no idea where I was going to stay or what I was going to do. About 20 miles from Grand Rapids, my car broke down. Great. Now I was homeless, jobless, and carless. I stood on the side of the highway, dejected. "Please God... I could really use a break." Just then a car pulled over, and an older gentleman asked if I needed help. I told him that I could use a ride to Aquinas College in Grand Rapids. "Hop in," he said.

When we arrived, I thanked the man and offered him some money for his trouble. He refused, but told me to remember to pay it forward. "Help the next guy when you get a chance." I would come to learn that this is how the people of Grand Rapids are. They give. For me, it was another lesson about the kind of man I wanted to be... the kind who would help people without expecting anything in return.

Joan drove me back to my car so I could get my things out of it, and we had it towed to the garage. I needed to figure out a place to stay, as sleeping on her couch in the dorm room wasn't fair to her roommates, or technically allowed. We talked about where I should stay, but were really quite uneducated in this department. Neither of us had ever rented an apartment before and had no idea where to start. I ended up finding a motel that rents rooms by the week for $210.

The money was starting to run low. I spent the next several weeks searching for a job, but had no luck. I really did not want to file for unemployment, but it was starting to look as though I had no choice. I have a thing about taking handouts. My family had been on welfare for much of my childhood, and it's a feeling that I don't like.

Our old friend Pat offered to let me stay at the house that she and a few of her classmates rented together, just until I could get some cash flow. I took her up on it and slept on their couch. This was getting old. I wanted a job... and a home.

A few weeks later, with the money almost gone and still no job offers, I reluctantly filed for unemployment. As soon as I got a check,

I rented a room for $50 a month from a guy named Hal. His house was in a pretty rough part of town, and although it wasn't a "home" to me, at least it was a place where I could sleep and hang my clothes.

I decided to go to an employment agency called Snelling and Snelling, which finds you a job and charges a percentage of your first year's salary. Joan had helped me compose a resume, and the people at the agency seemed impressed. I was told there'd be no problem finding me a job. The problem was going to be coming up with the money to pay them.

My thought was, let's see if I can get a job, then I'll worry about how to pay for it. Several interviews were set up within a week. Right off the bat I was offered positions as assistant manager at both Godfather's Pizza and Pizza Hut paying $18,000 a year. Part of me wanted to jump at the opportunity. That was pretty darn good money in 1983. But something told me to hold off. I had one more interview on Friday with a stock brokerage firm called H.B. Shaine & Co.

The position was for a mail clerk and runner and paid $12,500 a year. It involved many responsibilities, including picking up mail at 8 a.m., processing interoffice outgoing mail, inventory of office supplies, etc. The running part of the job sounded much more interesting. It involved delivering tens of thousands of dollars—sometimes hundreds of thousands—in stocks and bonds to firms in the Grand Rapids area. Being in communications in the Army, I had been entrusted with all kinds of confidential information, which made me a perfect candidate for the job. It was offered to me, and they wanted me to start on Monday! I told them I'd give them an answer by noon.

Joan and I had a lot to talk about. Do I take one of the higher-paying jobs with minimal opportunity for advancement, or do I take the lesser paying job? Joan said to me, "Well that depends, David. Do you want a career in the restaurant business? Or would you be more interested in moving up in the stock brokerage industry. Because to me, it sounds like there is a lot of room for growth there. Take the job that you think will make you happy."

I called H.B. Shaine and accepted the position. Then I went to the bank to ask for a loan, so I could pay for the job. We had to drive to Detroit to have my Uncle Bruce co-sign, but we got it done. Over the weekend, we went shopping for work clothes for me. It wasn't much, but I was able to get a few dress shirts, a few ties, some pants, and dress shoes.

On Monday morning, I reported for work and knew right away that I had made the right decision. It was exciting to learn about stocks, bonds, and the investment world. I knew that this could be a good career. When I looked at the brokers, I saw something that I wanted—a job they loved, and the ability to provide a comfortable living for their families. I knew that if I worked hard, I could have that, too. I now had a goal in life, and was more driven than ever.

Everything seemed to be falling in to place, except that Joan was finishing up her semester and would be going home to East Jordan for the summer. The day she was supposed to leave, a Friday afternoon, we were together and she drove me home. As we sat in the Chevette, it hit me like a ton of bricks that she was leaving. What if she went back home to East Jordan and decided that I really was not the one for her? What if she found someone else? What if she left and never came back?

All my life whenever I got close to someone or when things were going well for me, they seemed to find a way to fall apart. Everyone else in my life had abandoned me, why not her? I could not bear the thought of losing her. She made my life complete. I asked her not to go. "Stay with me," I pleaded.

"David, I can't. My parents would have a cow!" she laughed. Then she noticed that I wasn't laughing.

"Dave, you have nothing to worry about. I love you and that will never change. Besides, where would I live?"

I said, "We're engaged! You would stay here with me."

Joan was my best friend, my companion, my lover. She was everything to me, and I didn't want to spend a single day away from her. More important, I didn't want her to go home and realize that she didn't want me anymore.

Just then, the song, "When I'm With You" by Sherriff came on the radio. I was overcome by emotion and completely lost it. As the tears flowed, I tried one more time. "Please don't leave me."

I had never lost control over my emotions that way—certainly never in front of Joan. I was embarrassed, but the fear of being abandoned again took over. I think Joan understood, and it made our relationship even stronger.

She touched my hand and, for what seemed like an eternity, looked deep into my eyes. "Let me go home for the weekend and break this to my parents. I'll be back on Monday."

CHAPTER 13

Mrs. B.

When Joan returned from up north, she moved in to the tiny bedroom that I rented, and got a job through a temp agency working at ADAC Plastics. When she told her parents of her plans, and that she wouldn't be going back to school in the fall, they were not happy. Mostly, they were upset about her not finishing college. Joan hated the fact that she disappointed her parents.

Within a few weeks, we were able to get a place of our own. Joan found a two-bedroom duplex out in Allendale, about a 20-minute drive from Grand Rapids. Allendale was a very conservative Christian community; an unmarried couple living together would be frowned upon. When we first went out to look at the apartment, the landlord was reluctant to rent to us. He was a very devout Dutch Christian Reformed, and did not agree with cohabitation.

During the interview, we told him that we were engaged and trying to save for our wedding, and that we could not afford two separate apartments. He must have liked us, because he agreed to rent to us. He asked us to just be discreet and not advertise that we were living in sin. We paid the $295 deposit and the $295 first month's rent, and we had our first apartment!

Joan and I were so happy. We were in love and had our own place. Life was good. No, life was *great!* We went to church every Sunday and were starting to go to marriage class once a week. We only had one car though, because I sold my Buick Wildcat to some shady car dealer for $650 to pay for the apartment. Joan got a job at a bakery, which was closer to home than the factory. We hardly ever went out to eat or to movies or clubs, because we were saving for our wedding, but we had a great summer. We'd go to the Lake Michigan beaches in Grand Haven or Muskegon, or to festivals and just walk around or split a treat together. We always had fun, whether it was just staying home listening to Tiger baseball, playing board games or cards, washing the car, or working in the small garden we had behind the duplex.

Christmastime was magical. We didn't spend money on store-bought decorations, but made everything ourselves. Still, our tiny tree was beautiful. We were supposed to go up north for Christmas, but we were unable to make it due to a heavy snowstorm. It was just Joan and me on Christmas Eve, and I wouldn't have wanted to be anywhere else.

Joan waited until after I fell asleep, then quietly slipped out of bed and put my presents under the tree. Because she had hidden them throughout the apartment, I had no idea, and wasn't expecting anything. In the morning when we woke up, it looked as though Santa Claus had come. Never had I seen so many presents.

By this time, Joan and I were each working second jobs. Our wedding was just a few months away, and we needed to make as much money as possible to pay for it. I got a job at a shoe store in the mall, and Joan got a job at a pizza place.

Having only one car was a major inconvenience. I'd drop Joan off at the bakery at 6 a.m. and go to work at Shaine. At 2 p.m., she'd take the bus as far as it would go toward our apartment, then she'd walk the remaining 4 miles home. After a nap, she'd walk another 4 miles to the pizza place. After my day at the office, I worked in the shoe store until 9 p.m. Then I'd go to the pizza place and stay with Joan and help her close at 10 p.m.

When the weather started to turn colder, Joan would take the bus downtown after working in the bakery, and sit in the car until 5 p.m. when I got out. Then she would take me out to the mall and use the car to get to her second job. One of my co-workers gave me a lift from the mall to the pizza place. After several months of this, one of the brokers at Shaine who also owned a few bridal/tuxedo shops offered Joan a job. She was able to let go of her two part-time jobs and work at the bridal store full-time.

Life got a little easier, but Joan began to realize that she needed to go back to school. Working minimum-wage jobs was not the way we wanted to live our life. She applied to an accelerated nursing school program and was accepted. Our wedding was planned for Sat., July 28, 1984. Little did we know when we picked that date, that nursing school would start the following Monday. No honeymoon for us.

One of Joan's best friends, Aleda had an engagement party for us at her parent's house near Alpena, Mich. They had a place right on Lake Huron, and all of our friends came. We had so much fun! For me it was starting to sink in that this wedding was really going to happen... I was really going to marry the girl of my dreams.

Planning a wedding is a lot of work, but we sure had fun doing it. Joan made all of the flowers and decorations. We got a deal on both her dress and the tuxedos. Originally, we were going to get married in Grand Rapids, but decided to have it in East Jordan, at the church in which Joan was raised.

I stayed at The Jordan Inn the night before our wedding. I had a restless night and

Joan and me at Aleda's House – Spring 1983

could barely sleep. I finally got up around 6 a.m. and went for a walk down by the lake. It gave me a chance to reflect and think about how I had gotten to this point in my life... all the hard work and heartache. Ironically, it was the very same lakeside park where I played with my brother and sister while waiting for Neil to be interviewed by the Iron Works the first time we came to East Jordan.

I thought about my mother and my grandmother and wished that they could have been here to see that I had turned out to be a good man and that I was about to marry the most loving, thoughtful, caring, and beautiful woman in the world. I remembered eight years ago, being just a kid on this very same beach and falling in love with a girl named Joan. While walking along the shores of Lake Charlevoix, I remembered the feelings of inadequacy, of feeling inferior and not being accepted. Then I thought about the life ahead of me and got caught up in the emotion of it all.

After the tears subsided, I walked back to my room for a shower, and got ready for the best day of my life. I went out to eat with some friends, and then headed to the church. My mom's family all made the trip from southern Michigan to attend our wedding. It was great to see all of my aunts and uncles again. Jeff was my best man. Venzke came from Toledo, and my old buddy Tim came from Texas, to be in the wedding. Duane and Joan's brother were the other two groomsman. The Bees were our ushers.

Everybody I loved and cared about was here to celebrate this special day with us... everyone except my father, who we did not invite. It was my decision not to invite him. I didn't need the added worry of him starting a fight with my mom's family, Joan's family, or anyone else. He did that at Jeff's wedding. I figured that since he

was able to attend Jeff's wedding, my mom's family should be able to come to mine. I did feel bad about Kathy, though. I would have loved to see her and Mark again.

At 1 p.m., I stood at the front of the church and waited for my bride. I tried to remember to smile, as I could feel my heart skipping a few beats. Then I saw Joan. She looked so beautiful and so happy as she looked at me and walked toward me. "It's really going to happen," I told myself. I had to be the luckiest man on the face of the earth.

Our wedding – July 28, 1984

The rest of the day was a blur. There were so many people to visit with and catch up with. Many times someone would be talking to me, but I would become distracted... just looking at Joan as she mingled with the crowd. She was truly amazing. And now, finally, she was my wife.

I had booked a room for our wedding night at the Cadillac Sands, which was about 90 minutes away, heading toward Grand Rapids. At the reception, Joan and I decided that we didn't want to drive that far, and wanted to find a room a little closer along the way. The plan completely backfired. There were no rooms available... anywhere. Even the room we had book at the Cadillac Sands had been snapped up. We had no choice but to drive all the way home, arriving at 3 a.m.

The next day, Sunday, we moved into our new apartment in

Grand Rapids. It was hard to let go of our first home together, but it wasn't practical living so far from the city with just one car. The new apartment was not furnished, however, and we realized just how little we had. The move-in was easy, because we basically had nothing—no furniture, no bed, no kitchen table. We sat on our lawn chairs and slept on the floor. Still, we were very happy.

The next day, Joan started school. It didn't take long for us to figure out that there was no way that she could both work and go to school. She was in a 21-month accelerated nursing program, with only one-third of all students surviving until graduation. She quit her job and devoted all of her time to her studies.

I started my classes at Grand Rapids Junior College in September. Because it was only two classes to start out with, I decided to get another job. We had very little money and were just barely getting by. One night, when we had no food, we ate the top of our wedding cake from out of the freezer for dinner—the one couples traditionally eat on their first anniversary. (Hey, at least it was carrot cake.)

McDonald's was our salvation. The fast-food chain was running a promotion in conjunction with the 1984 Summer Olympics. Joan and I collected the game pieces, and when the United States got a gold medal, we won a free Big Mac; silver was an order of fries, and bronze was a drink. In 1984, Russia boycotted the Olympics. This eliminated much of the competition for the United States, and we won a ton of medals. Every time we redeemed a prize piece, we were given a free item that included yet another game piece. Joan and I just kept rolling our game pieces over and over and got many free McDonald's meals.

I ended up reenlisting in the Army, as a Reserve. I got a $1,800 bonus and $100 a month, which helped us pay for tuition and a few things for the apartment. I made an 18-month commitment, which would be up in January of 1986. Joan was on track to graduate in June of 1986. As a Reserve, my Army duties were one weekend a month, and two full weeks out of the year. On my first weekend of drill, I met a guy named Will Brabant. He was a local boy who played and loved hockey. We were inseparable during drill, and would spend extra time together outside of the Army. I liked to call him Willis.

In December, Joan's beloved grandmother passed away. She was devastated. Although I had a lot of experience in the loss department,

Joan did not. She was very close with her grandma, and her passing was very difficult. Unfortunately, this was only the beginning of the losses for Joan.

In the spring of 1985, I was promoted to the reorganization department at H.B. Shaine. I decided to take a full load of credit hours for the second quarter of school. Joan was so busy; there was really no reason for me not to stay just as busy. I worked from 8 .m. to 5 p.m., and took a class over the lunch hour, from 1-2 p.m. I had a four-hour class on Tuesday and Thursday nights from 6-10 p.m. Army Reserves was once a month on Saturday and Sunday from 8 a.m. to 5 p.m.

Although our lives had become extremely busy and harried, Joan and I were always there for each other. We tried to keep our Saturdays open to spend the day together. We would clean and do the laundry in the morning, and then the rest of the day was ours to do whatever we wanted. Sometimes, we would rent a video. We didn't have a VCR, so we would have to rent that, too. Other times, we just played music and cards or Trivial Pursuit.

The nursing program did not give spring or winter breaks, but in the summer Joan got three weeks off. Unfortunately, the break came at the same time as my two-week commitment to the Reserves. Willis and I were sent to California to Camp Roberts. The days dragged on. I missed Joan, and it killed me to know that we could have been spending these weeks together, with no worries about school.

The rest of the summer easily passed. It was nice to have a break from school; only working 45-50 hours a week and one weekend a month seemed like a breeze at this point. Mr. Shaine and I became very close. He was diabetic and not able to walk very far, so every morning I would wait by the curb for him to pull up, and then I would go park his car. He trusted me to drive his car, and he trusted me with his credit card to go and pick up his medication.

Mr. Shaine was a glider pilot in the 82nd Airborne Division in WWII, and loved to talk about his time in the service. He would frequently call me into his office just to chat. He was like a surrogate grandfather to me, always giving words of encouragement and advice, and always willing to help. His wife had died years ago, unexpectedly on the operating table, and he never remarried. I think he saw a lot of the way he felt about his wife when I talked about Joan.

For two-and-a-half years, I was the first person he saw in the morning and the last person he saw as he headed home. Mr. Shaine helped me pay for college, and asked to see my report cards each semester. Other than Joan, he was one of the few people in my life who believed in me. At Christmas, even though he was Jewish, he personally gave me a bonus, above and beyond what the firm gave me. After his wife died, he sold off several of his branches and donated $5 million dollars to medical research. I so admired his generosity, and knowing him and learning from him made me a better man.

In October of 1985, I was at drill with the Army Reserves on a Saturday. I was called to the Commander's office for an emergency phone call from my wife. I was really nervous to take the call, because Joan knew that I wasn't allowed to take phone calls at the Armory. It could be nothing but bad news. As I picked up the phone, I could hear Joan crying uncontrollably on the other end. "What's the matter?" I asked. "Pat died," she said.

"What?" I had no idea what she was talking about. "Somebody killed my sister!!"

I talked to my section Sergeant and was relieved from that weekend of duty. Once home, I tried to console Joan, but this was way out of my league. I knew how to help myself through the most difficult times, but I had never had to worry about someone else going through this kind of loss and was helpless. We threw some clothes in a suitcase, jumped in the car, and headed north. Joan was a wreck; I hated seeing her so hurt and upset. We didn't have any details about what had happened to Pat, but I wanted to personally take care of the person responsible.

When we arrived in East Jordan, it was just awful. Joan's parents were beside themselves. Pat was 32 years old and had two children. She had been murdered, and nobody knew by who, or why? Things like this didn't happen in East Jordan. Joan went into caretaker mode and did everything she could to comfort her mother and Pat's children.

The whole town was in shock. Going to the funeral home was very difficult, not only because I had no idea how to comfort Joan, but also because I hadn't been to the funeral home since my own mother died more than 10 years ago. I went off on my own, to the room where her funeral had been held, and just sat.

In the coming days, the man behind the horrendous crime was

revealed. It was some guy from town who really had been no part of any of our lives. He admitted to the murder, and even led the police to the dump to show them where he had hidden the weapon. Pat had not been raped, had not been robbed... she had been senselessly murdered for no apparent reason. The guy is in prison now—hopefully for the rest of his life. To this day, he has never said why he did it. Our family, and the small town of East Jordan, lost some of its innocence, and would never again be the same.

Fall and winter quickly passed. I finished up with my commitment to the Army in January, but Joan and I were still very busy with work and school. Mr. Shaine became too ill to work, confined to his home and requiring round-the-clock care. His personal assistant, Joyce, asked Joan to spend the night there and help take care of him five nights a week. I don't know how she managed to get through school on such little sleep.

One Saturday, we were sitting at the kitchen table doing homework. Joan got up and went into the bathroom. She seemed to be in there for a long time. When she came out, she had a look on her face that I had never seen before. I asked if everything was OK. She walked over to me, sat down, and looked into my eyes. "I think we are pregnant," she said.

I didn't know what to say. "How?" I asked.

"Really, do I need to tell you how?" Joan laughed.

"No, I mean how do you know?" I said.

She grabbed my hand and led me into the bathroom, where a pregnancy test sat on the counter. I picked it up and saw the positive sign. We just looked at each other and giggled nervously, and then hugged. We spent the evening talking about our future—our future as a family. Suddenly, there was a whole new outlook on life. I went to bed that night smiling and thinking, "I'm going to be a daddy."

Mr. Shaine passed away in April. He was such a kind soul, and a great mentor for me. I feel so very blessed to have known him. Before he died, he bought our new baby a silver piggy bank, which we still have. Joan applied for and received a position at the hospital where she went to nursing school. She would graduate on June 6th and start her new job two weeks later. Everything was perfect. We were in love, expecting our first child, Joan was going to be an

RN, and I was a year from getting my associates degree.

Joan's parents came down for her graduation. They were very proud, especially her mother, who was also in the medical profession. All Joan ever wanted to do was make her parents proud of her, and now it seems that she had. I, too, was very proud of her. I saw all of the hard work she put in to achieving her goal. Finally, it had paid off. Out of the 80 students who started the program, only 26 graduated.

About this time, one of my co-workers was going on vacation. He was the information tech guy who worked 11 p.m. to 8 a.m. and would be gone for two weeks. I was asked to cover his position while he was gone. So for two weeks I was working 16 hours a day. It was exhausting, but somehow I still managed to make it to my Tuesday night softball game.

I was playing center field that night. There was a runner on second with two outs. A grounder came through to my right. I ran over, picked up the ball, and threw a bullet to the plate to get the runner out. As I did so, I felt a little "pop" at the top of my head, followed by a stabbing pain. My face instantly felt hot, and by the time I made it back to the dugout, I had a tremendous headache.

I asked one of the guys to go to the car and ask my wife for some aspirin. Joan had been sitting out there crocheting a blanket for our new baby. The next thing I knew, Joan was in the dugout asking me what was wrong. I told her that I had a bad headache and asked if she could give me some aspirin. She said, "How bad is it on a scale of one to 10? Did it come on all at once, or have you had a headache all day?"

I told her that it happened suddenly and that it was very bad. She grabbed my stuff and said, "Let's go!"

"What?" I said.

"Now!! Let's go, David!"

By the time we got to the car, the pain had gotten even worse. Joan was speeding down the road, which she never does, and running red lights. I told her to pull over because I needed to throw up.

"I am not stopping," she said. "Do it on the floor."

She pulled up to the Emergency Room and helped me out. By this time, I was disoriented and babbling. I was immediately taken to a room and put on a gurney. I remember being so restless that I couldn't lay still. I was lying on the bed, and then would flip over the other way, throw off the covers and try to get up. The pain was so unbearable and I just wanted it to stop.

Joan kept telling me to lay still. She knew that she had to somehow get me to calm down and stay as still as possible, but I was thrashing from side to side in the bed. She came very close to me and put her hands on each side of my face. She told me to look at her, and then she said, "David, I need you to lay still. Every time you move around, it makes your blood pressure go up. You are bleeding in your brain. Listen to me, David. This is very serious. I need you to help me. I know it hurts sweetie, but please... just try to stay still." The next thing I knew, everything went black.

When I regained consciousness, I was in a long tube and my hands were restrained. I only opened my eyes for a second or two, and then I was out again. I don't remember a whole lot, but would spend three days in intensive care and four more in the neuro-trauma unit. (Ironically, this is precisely where Joan would start her new job in a week.)

As it turned out, I had a subarachnoid hemorrhage—a fancy way of saying that there was a bleed in my brain. Joan slept on a chair in the ICU and didn't leave my side until I woke up. Once I was stable, she went to the apartment to shower and make some phone calls. As she was driving, the song, "If You Leave" by OMD came on the radio. She started crying uncontrollably and had to pull over on the side of the road. I think it hit her all at once... if she had not acted as quickly as she did, or if she had not been there, I could have died.

We never learned what caused the bleed. It was assumed that it was an aneurysm, and it could rupture at any time. If this happened I could lose the functions of my body or motor skills, the ability to talk, walk, or worse. It was very frightening. Joan stopped at my work and talked to my boss, Ron. Later, she told me that she fell apart there too. After two angiograms, no aneurysm was ever found. My neurosurgeon told us that 98 percent of subarachnoid hemorrhages are caused by aneurysms. The other 2 percent are just spontaneous; I must just be one lucky SOB. He was a great doctor.

On the day I was to be discharged from the hospital, my head was clear, and I thought about everything that had happened. I thanked Joan. It was all because of her quick response that I was still alive.

If we had waited for an ambulance or done anything other than what she did, things could have been a lot worse. I think she got me to the hospital within 15 minutes of the onset of the bleed.

I told her, "I could have lost everything in a split second. I would never see you again. I would never see our new baby."

She looked back at me with tears in her eyes and said, "No, David. *I* could have lost everything."

CHAPTER 14

Family

The doctor told me to take a week off work, but I went back after just two days. I wanted to save my vacation time for when the baby came. Plus, I was feeling OK. Joan started her new job as an RN at St. Mary's Hospital. The rest of summer and early fall flew by, as we eagerly awaited the arrival of our first child. We moved into a larger apartment, and life was good.

At 2 a.m. on Oct. 22, 1986, Joan calmly woke me up from my sound sleep. "David, my water broke," she said. She had showered and was all ready to go to the hospital. The woman was amazing. I frantically leaped out of bed, and can only imagine how I must have looked. My mind was racing; I couldn't even figure out what I was supposed to be doing. Joan told me to calm down and take a shower. "We have time," she said.

"OK, OK, OK!!" I thought as I ran around.

Forty-five minutes later, we were in the car and heading to the hospital. I was running through the red lights and Joan said, "David, you don't have to run the lights."

"But I can!" I replied.

"Well I would really appreciate it if you didn't."

Our beautiful son was born via C-section later that afternoon. We named him Aaron Daniel Burch, and he was perfect. Joan had saved my life a few months ago, and now we had our first child. Joan had a few complications and had to stay in the hospital for a week. I just wanted my wife and child home! Finally, that time came.

Although I still had school, I took the week off work to be with them as much as possible. I was so happy and thankful for being blessed with first love of my life, and now the second love of my life, our son.

A few weeks later, my old buddy Willis was in town for drill and stopped over. We had frequently talked on the phone, but hadn't seen each other for a while. We had a good time catching up. Joan and I were happy to see him. The next weekend, my brother Jeff came to meet his new nephew. He and Vickie were living in Brooklyn, as he was in acting school. He was still in the Navy as an officer's cook and doing modeling part-time.

Our first Christmas as a family was wonderful. Although money was tight because we were saving for a house, Joan and I couldn't have asked for better gifts. We had each other... and we had our son.

After the holidays, we got really motivated to move and began looking for a house. In April, we learned that we were expecting our second child, and were thrilled. We found a house and moved in on June 1. I cut back to just three classes because our life was on such a fast track. I was 26 years old, had been married for three years, and couldn't help be marvel at how far we had come.

It seemed like just yesterday I was splitting a mayonnaise sandwich three ways with my brother and sister. And now here I was with a good job, a home, a wife who loved me as much as I loved her, one child and another on the way—a real family.

We spent the summer of 1987 making the house our own. We worked in the yard and turned one of the bedrooms into a nursery. The baby was due in January of 1988. I had purchased Mr. Shaine's 1974 Cadillac from his estate, so we finally had two cars. The economy was booming, and I was making my way up through the ranks at work.

H.B. Shaine had been under new management for more than two years. In June, the president and CEO, Ron Lemmon, resigned, as he thought the firm was taking on too much risk. The new owners were letting two of its brokers trade highly speculative and risky option contracts on the OEX (Standard & Poor's 100 index).

Lemmon felt the new owners were only interested in profits—not protecting Shaine's clients, employees, and assets from the increased risk associated with these option contracts, which could lead to massive losses.

As the summer turned in to fall, I was oblivious to this. Joan and I were feeling so good about our future. Aaron was coming up on his first birthday, and our new baby was due in just a few months.

On Friday, Oct. 16, 1987, the stock market took a huge hit, falling 108 points. At certain points during the day, it was down much more than that, but the market rallied and cut losses before the closing bell. On Monday, I arrived at work at 8 a.m. Management was on edge, as the S&P futures were signaling a huge decline at open and Asian markets had taken a beating overnight. The United States had bombed an Iranian oil platform in the Persian Gulf, and two leading banks had increased their prime lending rates.

The two aggressive brokers had written large contracts near the end of trading on Friday, expecting a rebound from that day's lows. This left Shaine and its clients exposed over the weekend. The market opened, and the Dow Jones was in a free fall. Shaine's management was in panic mode, trying to raise cash through pledging securities and trying to secure loans from banks and other brokerage firms. Our largest lender, Old Kent Bank, pulled its multimillion-dollar line of credit in an attempt to limit its own loss. Our firm's major shareholder, DST, would not give us the $2 million or so dollars we needed to stay open. By 4 p.m., when the closing bell rang, the market had fallen a record 508 points.

I went into my friend Randy's office (he was also my boss) and asked what was going on. He said, "We are done. Out of business." He asked me not to say a word to anyone and to report to work the next day as usual. I left his office, knowing he had a long night ahead of him.

The day would forever be remembered in American History as "Black Monday." Shaine could not meet its margin calls, and would suffer some $16 million dollars in losses.

The ride home was not pleasant. I was sick to my stomach, and so many things were running through my mind.

"Ron was right," I thought. "He tried to warn them, but they were more interested in profits... not protecting their clients or their employees."

"Poor Mr. Shaine. He worked all of his life to build this company... and now he's barely been dead a year, and the whole company is destroyed."

"What am I going to tell Joan? How will we pay our bills? I have a child, and one on the way... and now no income. Will I even get paid for the hours I've already worked this week?"

When I walked into the house, Joan came up to me and hugged me. She already knew what had happened; it had been all over the news. Word of our little brokerage firm, founded by a great man so many years ago, had made the national headlines.

I sat at the kitchen table, dumbfounded, as Joan held me.

"We're going to be alright, David," she whispered in my ear.

Friends and family members called to offer their condolences. It was as if someone had died. In fact, it felt as though Mr. Shaine had died all over again. Joan and I had both taken his death very hard, and now the death of the firm he had so proudly built and protected was almost too much to bear.

I remember Ron telling me last spring, right before he resigned, that Mr. Shaine would never have let this happen. He would not approve or subject his firm to this much risk. If only those in power would have listened.

The Securities Investor Protection Corp., New York Stock Exchange, and the Securities and Exchange Commission arrived late that night to close the doors and secure the firm's assets, in an attempt to protect our client's interests. I reported to work on Tuesday, as I was told to do. The authorities had us sign in, and then sent us home. We all met at a restaurant near the firm to talk.

Someone said that SIPC would be interviewing and hiring some Shaine employees to help in the liquidation of the firm's assets. They had found two Chicago brokerages to buy the firm. Rodmen and Renshaw Inc. would buy most of Shaine's assets, including its Grand Rapids headquarters and 4,500 customer accounts. Wayne Hummer & Co. would buy the firm's office in Aurora, Ill.

The CEO of Rodmen and Renshaw had been a personal friend of Mr. Shaine's and felt some obligation to him. He also saw a great opportunity; H.B. Shaine, a company that had been worth tens of millions of dollars, was sold for about $250,000.

Most of Shaine's employees chose to stay with Rodmen. A few of my friends and I went with SIPC. They offered us a 10 percent raise, and all of the benefits that we had at Shaine. I felt it was my best option. My goal at this point was to finish the semester at the junior college, and then focus on getting registered as a stockbroker.

Joan really wanted to go up north to spend Christmas with her family, but her doctor advised her to stay home, as she was so close to her due date. Her mom had not been feeling well, and Joan was desperate to be with her, but she decided to follow her doctor's orders.

On Christmas Day, Joan's mother, Mary, was admitted to the

hospital with severe back pain. After receiving the phone call, without hesitation, Joan began gathering our things and told me, "We have to go. I don't care what the doctor said, we *have* to go." She and her mother had a relationship like no other mother-daughter relationship that I have ever seen. They were incredibly close, and would do anything for one another.

At the hospital, the doctors were able to get Mary's pain under control and began running some tests. We couldn't stay long, but it was important to Joan that we were there. It meant a lot to her mother as well.

On Dec. 29, 1987, Joan was scheduled for a C-section. We were so excited about the arrival of our second child. Halfway through the surgery, Joan informed the doctor that she could feel what they were doing. "I can feel you cutting me!" she exclaimed. "That's impossible," the doctor said. "You've had a spinal; everything should be numb." Then Joan started moving her legs and everybody knew this was not good.

The next 10 or 15 minutes were just horrible, as the surgical team tried to get the baby out as quickly as possible. It was horrifying to watch my wife in so much pain, and so helpless to do anything about it. All I could do is sit by her side and hold her hand and try to take her mind off of what was happening. She was a trooper though, and once again she amazed me with her strength. Our son, Jacob Phillip Burch, was born healthy and strong, and we couldn't have been happier.

Within a month, we received the news that Mary had cancer. Joan was devastated and took the news very hard. Being a nurse, she knew that the prognosis was not good for multiple myeloma. The average life expectancy at that time was 17 months. She would take baby Jake and go up north to be with her mother as often as she could. I'd keep Aaron home with me to make things a little easier for her. Often times, Joan would work a 12-hour shift overnight, and then make the three-hour drive to East Jordan. Mary had surgery to remove what tumors they could, and then started chemotherapy and radiation.

I started studying at night for the Series 7 exam, which I needed to pass in order to become a stockbroker. It was a tough test; a large percentage of those who take it failed on the first try. Of those who succeeded, most were college graduates at the top of their classes. Here I was, a sub-par high school student, and a college student with a 2.75 GPA. I was very nervous to take the test.

I was working full-time and had two young children, and a wife who also worked full-time. So much of my studying came late at night, into the early morning, and on the weekends. I studied hard and remained focused, though, knowing that I only had one shot at passing the exam.

The test was to be held in Detroit. I went a day early and stayed in a hotel so I could do some last-minute cramming. Back then, the exam was on paper and written with a No. 2 pencil—and no calculators. I took three pencils with me, just in case. I felt good after taking the test, but it would take four weeks to get the results.

Needless to say, those four weeks were very nerve-wracking. But a letter finally arrived in the mail. With my hands shaking, I carefully opened the envelope with a letter-opener and took out the paper inside. I had passed! *"Holy crap! I passed!"*

A small investment firm in Grand Rapids called Peninsular Securities, which happened to be in the same building that H.B. Shaine had occupied, hired me. It was very difficult to have a job that paid on commissions only. I opened my first account within three days of cold-calling, then another, then another. My first paycheck from Peninsular for the month of July was a whopping $278 dollars—$278 for an entire month's work. That averaged out to about $1.70 an hour. August was not much better, and I was beginning to wonder how we were going to make ends meet.

Joan and I found out in October that we were expecting our third child and were very excited. We wanted our children to be close in age. Aaron and Jake were 14 months apart, and there would be 17 months between Jake and the new baby. It also meant that we would have three in diapers at the same time. Yikes. I needed to make more money.

Joan asked me if I thought I made the right decision to work at Peninsular. They didn't have good benefits, and they were a little-known firm. Finally, I decided to start looking at other options. I had a few clients by then, maybe someone else would hire me. I sent resumes to Paine Webber, Prudential Securities, Merrill Lynch,

AG Edwards, and Shearson Lehman Hutton.

I had interviews with all of them except Merrill Lynch, which did not interview people without a bachelor's degree. That really got my dander up. "I already have clients and I am registered!" I thought. The other firms gave me interviews and had me take a battery of tests; they also arranged phone interviews with executives in New York. I received offers from two firms, but I really wanted to work for Shearson Lehman Hutton. The office manager there was a man named Bud Lucas; he was an old-time broker who told it exactly the way it was.

The first time I met Bud he was working as the branch manager of what was then called E.F. Hutton & Co. I was the runner at H.B. Shaine and had some bonds to deliver. Bud signed for them. We got to chatting, and he asked me where I grew up. I told him East Jordan and Trenton. As it turned out, he had friends in Trenton and told me their names. "I used to date their daughter in eighth grade," I told him. "What a small world."

I would have many more deliveries to E.F. Hutton during the Shaine years and talked to Bud each time. We always seemed to hit it off.

Bud told me about an excellent training program that they had. The problem was that I had to score high on the IQ test. I told him that I was a terrible test-taker and that I didn't think that I'd do well. He encouraged me to go ahead and take it anyway—and that he'd hire me either way. If I passed, then I would go into the training program. If not, he'd hire me outright. I'd be paid $2,000 per month plus commissions for the first six months. After that, no salary—just commissions.

I took the test the last week of December. The results would not be in until the first week of January. We set my final interview for that week.

After what seemed like an eternity, it was time for my appointment with Bud. I felt good about the personality test, but was concerned about the IQ test. When I entered Bud's office, he was sitting at his desk with two pieces of paper in front of him. He picked up the papers, one in each hand and then turned his back to me as he swiveled in his chair. I was a nervous wreck as I sat there and waited.

Suddenly and swiftly, he spun back around in his chair and looked me in the eye. "David, according to this IQ test, you are a freaking moron! Well not a moron, just not the IQ we look for in our advisors. On the other hand, I have never in all my years, seen a higher score on a personality test." As I sat there, speechless, he said, "However, a deal is a deal. You do not qualify for the training program, but I will hire you outright. Do not make me look like a fool!"

I told him, "I promise I will not disappoint you."

I was hired in January of 1989. I started slowly, but little by little began to build momentum. I worked from 7:30 a.m. to 5 p.m. Monday-Friday. Tuesday through Thursday, I also worked in the evenings from 7-9 p.m., and then on Saturdays I worked from 9 a.m. to 3 p.m. Most of that time I spend cold calling. We needed to make 100 contacts per day on top of handling our regular business. I was opening five or six accounts per month, but I needed to do better. Then in May, I landed a $5 million dollar account and Bud was ecstatic. He told me that he was very proud of me, and that he had seen a drive in me that was rare.

Although we were excited about the arrival of our new baby, the condition of Joan's mother was rapidly deteriorating. We went up to East Jordan as often as we could as a family, but Joan frequently went up by herself to help take care of her mom. It was clear that the end was near.

Because of the traumatic experience during the delivery of our son Jake, Joan was terrified to go through another C-section. Luckily, she had become friends with one of the anesthesiologists at work, who agreed to be there on the day of the delivery and take good care of her. We attended the same church, and she completely trusted him. He told her that he remembered a time a little over a year ago, when the hospital had received a bad batch of medication and the same thing had happened to a few other patients. He promised that he wouldn't let anything like that happen to her again.

On the morning of May 18, 1989, without any complications whatsoever, Joan gave birth to our daughter, Lindsay Mary Burch. Joan never looked more radiant as she did while holding our beautiful baby girl. Although it was among the happiest times of our lives, it was bittersweet, because Joan's mom was dying. The hospital stay was cut short so that we could get back up north. The day Joan and the baby were discharged, we left the hospital, went home to pack, and then went directly to East Jordan.

When we arrived, Mary was sitting in her chair, resting. Joan walked in with our daughter in her arms, and knelt down before her mom. "Mumma? This is your new granddaughter," Joan said. "Her name is Lindsay Mary."

Mary reached with her hand and gently stroked the baby's head. Then she looked up at Joan and smiled.

Soon after, Mary slipped into a coma. Six weeks later, she passed away. Joan was inconsolable. It broke my heart to see her in pain, and I did everything I could to help her through it. Before long, Joan started to get back to her old self. Her life experiences and losses had molded her into an incredibly strong and compassionate woman, mother, nurse, and wife.

My career soon caught fire, and in September of that year, I had my first really good month, grossing more than $15,000. In April of 1991, I opened 22 accounts and brought in more than $3 million dollars. Within a year, I brought in $15 million in assets. I was moved out of the cubicles and given my own office. In the brokerage industry, this is a big deal. Getting your own office means the firm believes in you and wants you to stay.

Me, Joan, Aaron, Lindsay, & Jacob - 1997

After moving in to my new space, I took a moment to reflect upon my life… the struggles I had faced… the pain I endured… the people who helped me along the way. I thought about the miracle of finding and loving Joan… having that love returned… our three amazing children.

And it suddenly struck me: The success I had been searching for, the love and security I had longed for my entire life—was now mine. I had arrived.

Epilogue

Joan and I were both dedicated to being the best parents that we could possibly be. When the kids were young, especially because they were so close in age, they took up most of our time. But we never put our own relationship on the back burner.

Although we rarely went out, we made a point to spend alone time together after the children went to bed. Sometimes we played cards or games or watched a movie. Sometimes we talked for hours; sometimes we sat next to each other and said nothing at all.

In March of 1991, I received a phone call from the father of my close friend Will Brabant. He told me that Willis had been killed in a construction accident. I was heartbroken. Willis had just gotten married and had a 6-month-old son. Now he was gone. It brought me back to 1986 when Joan had to rush me to the hospital, and how lucky I was to have survived.

A few years later, my sister Christina would succumb to an addiction to prescription drugs. She left behind three young boys.

I am now 51 years old and have spent most of my life in the financial services industry, starting when I was 22 years old. I have made millions of dollars over the last 29 years. Our children went to excellent schools and all played travel hockey. We live in an upscale area of Grand Rapids. I'm still blissfully married to the woman I fell in love with on a small beach in East Jordan all those years ago.

These are not the words of an arrogant man; they're the words of an extremely blessed man. However, my success did not come without pain and sacrifice. The pain I encountered as a child runs very deep, and although it has eased with time—and the love and support of others—it has never completely gone away.

I could have given up in 1967 when my father was taken away. I could have given up when my mother did not return home in 1974. I could have stayed in Trenton in 1976, and lost myself to drugs and alcohol. I had every reason to not join the Army or wait for Joan. I could have listened to the people who told me that I'd never amount to anything... or believed the tests I took in school that told me that my best career option was general labor. I could have kept working at that gas station in Charlevoix.

Joining the Army was one of the toughest decisions I ever had to make—even harder than the decision to run away from home after the 9th grade. But without the Army, I never would have learned how to respect myself or earn the respect of others. The Army changed my life in every possible way. It made me a man.

I am convinced that without the Army, Joan and I would never have married. She saw in me a boy that she liked a lot, perhaps even loved. But the boy had many issues and no direction. She watched that boy become a man, and each time he came home on leave, her feelings of love deepened. Ultimately, she wrote him a letter that would forever change both of their lives.

In life there are good times and bad times… triumphs and adversities… mountains to climb and plateaus to enjoy. The truth is—you don't have to settle for the cards you have been dealt. Rearrange your hand and look at your options.

We are not all born into privilege, but that doesn't mean that we are less deserving. And great privilege doesn't always bring happiness.

Some of my fondest memories are of when Joan and I had nothing… eating the top of our wedding cake for a meal because we had no other food, sitting on lawn chairs in our living room because we had no other furniture, praying that the United States would win a gold medal so we could redeem our game piece for a free Big Mac from McDonalds.

Heck, I even think about having a mayonnaise sandwich every now and then.

I have carried three things in my wallet for more than 30 years. The first thing is my student ID from second grade. Looking at the picture of me as a little boy reminds me of the pain and the hunger I endured every day of my life that year.

The second is the military dog tag that belonged to Mr. Edward Brzozowy. He was a Marine in the early 1960s. He gave it to me while I was working at The Country House, his bar and restaurant. He told me that he had hoped to give it to his son someday, but he never had one. He said that if he had had a son, he would want him to be like me. He asked me to keep the dog tag and know that he was proud of me. He knew what a challenging life I had.

The third item I have kept is a short essay I picked up while in the Army. Written by the Christian pastor Chuck Swindoll, it's simply titled, "Attitude."

> *The longer I live, the more I realize the impact of attitude on life. Attitude, to me, is more than facts. It is more important than the past, than education, than money, than circumstance, than failures, than successes, than what other people think or say or do.*
>
> *It is more important than appearance, giftedness, or skill. It will make or break a company... a church... a home. The remarkable thing is we have a choice every day regarding the attitude we will embrace for that day. We cannot change our past... we cannot change the fact that people will act in a certain way. We cannot change the inevitable.*
>
> *The only thing we can do is play on the one string we have, and that is our attitude. I am convinced that life is 10 percent what happens to me and 90 percent how I react to it. And so it is with you... we are in charge of our attitudes.*

The important thing to remember is this: We all have dreams. Don't settle—and don't stop until you have everything you want.

You deserve it.

About the Author

David B. Burch is an executive in the financial services industry. He and his wife live in Michigan, where they're the proud parents of three grown children and grandparents of twin boys. This is David's first book.

www.davidbburch.com

Topics for Discussion

1. What is the significance of the title, "Pocket Full of Dreams"? Would you have given the book a different title? If so, why?

2. In your opinion, what scene was the most pivotal? How would the story have changed without that scene?

3. What surprised you the most about the book?

4. What scene resonated most with you personally?

5. Which characters did you like the most/least and why?

6. What specific themes did the author emphasize throughout the book?

7. How do the characters change or evolve throughout the course of the story? What do you think triggered such changes?

8. Several characters faced choices that had moral implications. What were some of them? Would you have made the same decisions? Why or why not?

9. What lesson(s) do you think the author is hoping to convey by sharing his story? What was your biggest takeaway?

10. Did the book end the way you expected?